TOWARD AN END TO HUNGER IN AMERICA

TOWARD AN END TO HUNGER IN AMERICA

Peter K. Eisinger

BROOKINGS INSTITUTION PRESS
Washington, D.C.

$BMM5838 - 5/3$

ABOUT BROOKINGS

The Brookings Institution is a private nonprofit organization devoted to research, education, and publication on important issues of domestic and foreign policy. Its principal purpose is to bring knowledge to bear on current and emerging policy problems. The Institution maintains a position of neutrality on issues of public policy. Interpretations or conclusions in publications of the Brookings Institution Press should be understood to be solely those of the authors.

Copyright © 1998

THE BROOKINGS INSTITUTION
1775 Massachusetts Avenue, N.W., Washington, D.C. 20036

Library of Congress Cataloging-in-Publication data

Eisinger, Peter K.
    Toward an end to hunger in America / Peter K. Eisinger.
    p. cm.
    Includes bibliographical references and index.
    ISBN 0-8157-2282-6 (cloth : alk. paper)
    ISBN 0-8157-2281-8 (pbk. : alk. paper)
    1. Food relief—United States.   2. Hunger—United States.   I.
Title.
    HV696.F6 E47 1998   98-25392
    363.8'83—ddc21   CIP

9 8 7 6 5 4 3 2 1

The paper used in this publication meets the minimum requirements of the American National Standard for Information Sciences—Permanence of Paper for Printed Library Materials, ANSI Z39.48-1984

Typeset in Adobe Garamond

Composition by
R. Lynn Rivenbark
Macon, Georgia

Printed by
R. R. Donnelley and Sons
Harrisonburg, Virginia

Acknowledgments

I wrote most of this book at the La Follette Institute of Public Affairs at the University of Wisconsin–Madison, though final revisions were completed at my new institution, Wayne State University's College of Urban, Labor and Metropolitan Affairs. The project took a good part of the decade of the 1990s, during which time the La Follette Institute provided constant support and stimulation. It is a wonderful place to work. For one thing, the institute provided me with summer support and travel grants to pursue my research. In addition, it paid for a small army of graduate research assistants, including, in more or less chronological order from the very beginning of the project, Chris Stangel, Kristin Stout, Vicki Flood, Brett Desnoyers, Chad Reuter, and Armando Mota. I am grateful for their conscientious help. I also benefited from a La Follette institution, the Public Affairs Workshop, or PAWS, a faculty seminar devoted to dissecting works in progress. Nearly all my La Follette colleagues attended these sessions, and no one was shy about suggesting how to improve the research under discussion. Bob Haveman, Karen Holden, Karl Kronebusch, Andrew Reschovsky, John Karl Scholz, and Michael Wiseman were particularly helpful. I am grateful as well to the Graduate School at the University of Wisconsin for providing a semester's research leave during the course of my writing.

Several other people read and commented on parts of the manuscript, including Erica Eisinger, who made a crucial suggestion at the revision stage, Dick Merelman and Jane Voichik at Wisconsin, Christine Olson at Cornell, Gary Bickel at USDA, Kathryn Porter at the Center on Budget and Policy Priorities, and Larry Brown and John Cook at Tufts University. The latter two scholars graciously opened the files of the Tufts Center on Hunger, Poverty and Nutrition Policy to me in the summer of 1995. I also want to thank Representative Tony Hall's staffers, Jennifer Coken and Max Finberg, for making available to me the archives of the House Select Committee on Hunger.

Alice Honeywell, an old friend, edited the manuscript with her usual circumspect care, which I appreciate. Finally, I want to thank the Brookings editorial people—Nancy Davidson, Janet Walker, and Susan Woollen—for their support, good judgment, and nice design sense.

For Erica

Contents

Notes   135

Index   169

Tables

TOWARD AN END TO HUNGER IN AMERICA

1 | *The Problem of Hunger in the United States*

When the flush of holiday goodwill inevitably fades in the months after the new year, private donations by religious congregations and service clubs to food pantries in the United States begin to dwindle. Yet even as the pantries struggle to replenish their food stocks, demand remains high. Hungry people are hungry in every season.

Their numbers are substantial. Americans have known about the existence of hunger in a general way for a long time, but figures released by the federal government in the fall of 1997 provide the first reliable national estimate of the specific dimensions of hunger in the United States.[1] Based on a battery of questions asked by the Census Bureau in its Current Population Survey (CPS) in April 1995, a federal interagency task force estimates that 4.16 million households containing more than 11 million people could be classified as "food insecure with hunger," a category that includes those households in which at least one member had experienced hunger within the preceding twelve-month period.[2] An additional 7.8 million households containing more than 23 million people were classified as "food insecure without hunger." This is a condition in which there is no actual hunger in the household but the respondent expresses "concerns about the adequacy of the household food supply and report[s] some adjustments to dietary intake" because of lack of sufficient money.[3] These

1

figures combined suggest that food insecurity with its various levels of severity, which we will refer to for simplicity's sake as the "hunger problem," afflicts almost 12 percent of all American households, even in the relatively prosperous years at the end of the twentieth century.

Why is it that so many Americans are hungry? Why are so many at risk of hunger? It is not as though there is not enough food to go around in the United States. The famines common in less developed parts of the world, brought on by civil wars and crop failures, are unknown here. Abundance is so commonplace that American consumers, retailers, and restaurants throw away more than a quarter of the food stock every year.[4] American farmers not only produce more than enough for the domestic population, but they also feed the world: the United States leads in the export of wheat and corn by far, and ranks third in the export of rice.[5] Food is also cheap in the United States. American consumers spend a smaller percentage of their personal income on food—only 7.7 percent in 1993—than any other people on earth.[6] For these proportionally modest expenditures, Americans are still able to consume on a per capita basis more calories a day than people in virtually any other country.[7]

Nor is it enough to explain the persistence of various levels of food insecurity in the United States by arguing that it is simply an artifact of poverty. Certainly those who are hungry are generally poor. Food insecurity is in fact defined as lack of steady access to sufficient food because of financial "resource constraint."[8] But there is no one-to-one correspondence between food insecurity and income: the relationship is more complex. The 1995 CPS data show that nearly 70 percent of the respondents with incomes below the federal poverty line have access to sufficient and decent food on a regular basis and can thus be classified as "food secure." Hunger itself was most prevalent among those with incomes less than half the poverty line, but even among this poorest group of respondents only about 16 percent reported that someone in their household had experienced hunger. Almost 60 percent of these very poor households fell in the "food secure" category.[9]

The fact that most poor people, including even the poorest of the poor, do not experience food insecurity suggests that this society has ways to protect people without financial resources from hunger. In fact a host of public and private programs are devoted to this end, and their administrators know that combating food insecurity is, at one level, no more complex than making sure that needy people have easy access to food on a regular basis. As the 1997 Department of Agriculture (USDA) report suggests, "If the household . . . receives food assistance, the household's degree of food insecurity or hunger would presumably be reduced."[10] Hunger is, in other words, a tractable problem: we know its cure. It is tractable not only because we know what we need to end the hunger problem but also because no one has any interest in its perpetuation. Food insecurity is not a complex social problem whose solution requires a significant change in certain behaviors of those who experience it. In this regard, hunger differs from problems such as drug use, teen pregnancy, crime, or AIDS. Individuals engaging in substance abuse or unprotected sex or crime may derive pleasure or profit from these socially and self-destructive acts. Thus solutions must work against the short-term impulses (or the uncontrollable addiction) of the perpetrators or victims themselves. But the hungry are different. They willingly embrace the solution to their condition: regular access to sufficient food.

Thus the question remains: Why are so many Americans hungry or at risk of hunger? Given vast American abundance as well as the comparative simplicity of the solution to hunger, why has American society failed to eliminate the problem? "We are unique among all the nations in the history of the world," observed Representative Leonard Farbstein (D-N.Y.) during the debate in the 1960s over the establishment of a permanent food stamp program, "in that we are plagued with the problem of being able to grow too much food for our people rather than too little. And yet a full one-fifth of our people are not able to obtain sufficient of the proper foods to eat decently."[11] This is the puzzle that this book explores.[12]

The Presumption of Abundance

Hunger in America is a puzzle in part because Americans have generally taken for granted the availability of abundant food while they also have believed that they were under a certain moral obligation to share their own abundance. This has been the case almost from the beginning. By the time Robert Beverley, an amateur colonial historian, wrote his history of Virginia in 1705, his portrayal of America as the garden of the world was already a "stock image."[13] Yet its power was such that this depiction persisted as a literary theme long beyond the initial settlement period. "Here," wrote Crèvecoeur in his *Letters from an American Farmer* (1782), "nature opens her broad lap to receive the perpetual accession of new comers, and to supply them with food."[14] Tocqueville, too, was impressed by the abundance and accessibility of nature's gift to the Americans: "The territory of the Union presents a boundless field to human activity, and inexhaustible materials for labor. . . . The heat of faction is mitigated by a consciousness of prosperity."[15]

If the early European explorers and settlers saw the new world as a place of extraordinary fertility and abundance, so too do the modern inhabitants of the United States. In the realm of popular culture there is no more familiar icon of American bounty than Norman Rockwell's famous *Freedom from Want* painting. Adopted by the federal government in 1943 for use as both domestic and overseas wartime propaganda, the picture is said to be among the most reproduced and widely distributed paintings in the world.[16] This sentimental rendering of a Thanksgiving dinner features an ordinary family, gathered around the harvest table, whose centerpiece is a turkey of immense proportions. In other societies, a bird of these dimensions, if it were available at all, might cost a month's salary or more. Yet in America abundance is, as David Potter once argued, a "basic condition of American life."[17]

One response to this overwhelming abundance has been for Americans to hold the moral conviction that they have an obligation to share. During the debate over the food stamp program, for example, Representative William Ryan (D-N.Y.) commented, "As long as we have food surpluses and hungry people, it is immoral to keep the surpluses from needy families."[18] Or as Representative Bill Emerson (R-Mo.), a longtime supporter of food assistance programs, put it nearly twenty-five years later during another debate over food stamp funding, "There's a feeling that in a nation of abundance, where there is surplus food and, indeed, wasted food, that no one should go hungry."[19]

The duty to share our abundance has consistently been articulated at the highest level of national politics. John F. Kennedy played on this theme in the first televised campaign debate with Richard Nixon. "This is a great country," Kennedy said, "but I think it could be a greater country." Then he spoke of billions of dollars of surplus food, some of which lay rotting; of 4 million Americans dependent on surplus commodities worth no more than a nickel a day; and of West Virginia schoolchildren who took part of their school lunches home to feed their families. "I don't think we are meeting our obligations toward these families," he concluded.[20] On taking office Kennedy initiated a pilot food stamp program. Lyndon Johnson, under whom food stamps became permanent, later declared, "We want no American in this country to go hungry. We believe that we have the knowledge, the compassion, and the resources to banish hunger and to do away with malnutrition if we only apply those resources and those energies."[21]

Republican presidents as well viewed the problem of hunger through a moral prism. For Nixon, the presence of hunger was a source of national shame. "We have long thought of America as the most bounteous of nations," he said in a message to Congress in 1969 that set into motion plans for a White House conference on food and hunger. "So accustomed are most of us to a full and balanced diet that, until recently, we have thought of hunger and malnutrition as problems only in far less fortunate countries. [But now] there can be no doubt that hunger and malnutrition exist in America, [a situation] embarrassing and intolerable, [where] the honor of American democracy is at issue."[22] Similarly, for Ronald Reagan's Task Force on Food Assistance it was "an article of faith among the American people that no one in a land so blessed with plenty should go hungry. . . . Hunger is simply not acceptable in our society."[23]

The articulation by political leadership of a national obligation to banish hunger is matched to a large extent by attitudes among the public. Janet Poppendieck, a historian of the depression-era commodity assistance programs, sees this sense of moral duty with respect to food as a general cultural trait. She writes, "The norms and values violated by the existence of hunger" in the United States—norms of sharing and compassion—are "widespread and deeply felt."[24] National survey data generally show strong support for food assistance to the hungry. Robert Shapiro and his colleagues report a national poll in which 71 percent of respondents support the proposition that "the federal government has a deep responsibility for seeing to it that . . . no one goes hungry." In another survey 94 percent agreed with the statement that "it's not right to let people who need welfare go hungry."[25] Still other polls find a willingness among a majority of respondents to pay more in taxes in order to increase spending on federal food programs.[26] This fund of public support for government food assistance makes the question of why we have not solved the hunger problem all the more puzzling.

Solving the Hunger Puzzle

This study is organized around a series of questions, the answers to which should lead to solving the puzzle. These questions explore the general proposition that the perception of hunger and our responses to it emerge from a complex intellectual, political, and social context.[27]

Although our impulse as a society and as individuals is to be generous and compassionate, it is not so simple to realize this impulse fully in policy or practice. Each of these contextual elements has built-in contradictions and weaknesses, not the least of which is endemic public suspicion of public welfare. These contradictions work against simple generosity and render easy policy solutions difficult. Consider then the following questions:

Have we failed to eliminate food insecurity because we have not in fact been able to understand the nature of the problem? For the purposes of crafting public policy, understanding may be regarded as a function of both definition and measurement. The issues of how we define and measure hunger constitute the intellectual context of the hunger puzzle. Neither task has been simple. Clearly, if we have not been able to understand the exact nature of the problem that we seek to address, then our policy tools may be poorly designed or misguided. Then, to the extent that we have not been able to agree on how to measure the problem, we have no sure way of establishing its magnitude.

Chapter 2 addresses the search for a meaningful definition of hunger, one that captured the nature of food deprivation in a society characterized by widespread abundance. Notions of hunger that derived from the experiences of third world societies dealing with famine, in which scarcity, starvation, wasting, and diseases like kwashiorkor are common, came quickly to be seen as inadequate for understanding how Americans experienced hunger. Yet for a long time, hunger was equated with malnutrition. Eventually, however, analysts turned away from physiological symptoms as the key to understanding hunger in America and began to develop the sociological notion of food insecurity to describe the nature of food deprivation in a wealthy society.

At the same time that the struggle to define the hunger problem was occurring, policy analysts both in and out of government were attempting to gauge the magnitude of the problem. Chapter 3 presents the history of hunger measurement that eventuated in the CPS report of 1997.

The argument of these chapters on the intellectual context in which the hunger problem has been understood is that after three decades the policy community has at last achieved a certain consensus on the nature of food deprivation and its prevalence. The difficulty of arriving at this consensus, however, has to this point been an impediment to confronting the hunger problem effectively.

Have we failed to solve the hunger problem because we do not have good or sufficient policy tools? The federal government maintains nearly a dozen different food assistance programs, which cost taxpayers close to $39 billion in 1997. Food assistance consumes almost half the entire USDA budget. The food stamp program is an entitlement for virtually all low-income Americans, while the remaining programs are targeted at especially vulnerable subgroups in the poverty population, including infants, pregnant women, schoolchildren, and the elderly. Nevertheless, the magnitude of this effort aside, it seems logical to suspect that if millions of Americans are hungry, then something must be wrong with the policy tools.

Chapters 4 and 5 explore the origins and operations of the major federal food assistance programs. The analysis concludes that the design of the federal policy effort—a broad entitlement supplemented by smaller targeted initiatives—is strong. Public food assistance, however, rests on the pivot point between American society's compassion for the hungry and its suspicion of public welfare and welfare recipients. The consequence is that the programs have often been administered in ways that are punitive and grudging, restricting eligibility and imposing a stigma that many are not willing to bear. In addition, the programs have been chronically underfunded. The result is that for many people, both enrollees and the merely eligible, federal food assistance is inadequate to prevent food insecurity.

Have we failed to solve the hunger problem because the issue has never commanded more than a marginal place on the congressional agenda? Although many members of Congress have been eloquent in their articulation of the society's moral obligation to feed the hungry, the federal food assistance effort has largely been the responsibility of agriculture committees without a primary interest in poverty policy and of temporary select committees without full legislative powers. Although the select committees were able to focus attention on the hunger problem, they were in the end institutionally and politically weak devices for representing the interests of a powerless constituency. Chapter 6 explores the history in particular of the Senate Select Committee on Nutrition and Human Needs in the 1970s and the House Select Committee on Hunger established in 1983. Both committees were terminated by their respective houses before their members thought their work was finished, leaving congressional hunger relief advocates without an institutional base in the legislative body.

Have we failed to solve the hunger problem because the advocacy community is weak? At first glance the community of interest groups working on behalf of food assistance and the hungry appears too fragmented to present a forceful common front. But a more careful examination in chapter 7 suggests that the various groups have worked out an implicit division of labor in pursuit of advocacy for the hungry. They manage as well to present a cohesive stance by coordinating their efforts through an informal "executive committee" of the community. The failure to solve the hunger problem cannot be attributed to shortcomings of the interest group community, which appears to have worked out the means to maximize the weight of its modest resources.

Have we failed to solve the hunger problem because so much of the task of food assistance has been delegated to the nonprofit volunteer sector? Volunteer organizations from both the religious and secular communities are important not only as advocates for the hungry but also as vehicles for delivering both private and public food aid. Soup kitchens, food pantries, and commodity distribution centers feed millions of people every year. Yet in certain important respects, the volunteer sector is inadequate to the task. It cannot compensate for downward fluctuations in federal food assistance, and it cannot offer consistent help in every season.

Nevertheless, the private sector effort to feed the hungry has widespread legitimacy in the United States, and it successfully mobilizes the energies of a vast number of ordinary people. In the final chapter, I argue that solutions to food insecurity rest finally on tapping these virtues and creating a stronger partnership between private and public food programs.

2 | *Defining Hunger*

Most Americans probably do not worry much about how to define hunger in any technical way: ordinary people and even health professionals often think they know it when they see it.[1] The skeletal bodies of third world victims of war and crop failure who occasionally appear on our television screens are living and dying proof of hunger. So too, in a far less extreme way, are the crowds of street people waiting in line at private soup kitchens in American towns and cities.

Not only do people think they know hunger when they see it, but they apparently make distinctions about its severity and incidence. The hunger in foreign lands to which Americans respond with planeloads of foodstuffs is perceived as different from the hunger of Americans themselves. The former is life-threatening; it produces refugees; it destroys societies. The latter is a personal crisis, rarely lethal, for a certain limited number of people. It is a national embarrassment but no threat to an otherwise stable and prosperous society. Foreign hunger typically occurs under conditions of extreme scarcity; American hunger occurs in a land of widespread abundance.

Valid as these perceptions and distinctions are, however, they do not constitute an adequate basis to define the object of policy. Yet members of the policy community interested in food assistance were not able for a long time to achieve consensus on a definition of hunger that was useful for policymaking.[2]

The issue of definition is critical. For one thing, definition provides the theoretical basis for the development of operational or measurement indicators.[3] No census or estimate of the prevalence of the problem is possible without knowing exactly what it is that is to be counted and what is to be excluded. We cannot know how many hungry people there are until we have defined hunger in such a way that we can reliably sort people into "hungry" and "not hungry" categories.

Furthermore, as David Dery points out, definition is important because it underwrites our collective responses. "Problems are . . . defined," he writes, "so as to guide future policy. . . . Problem definition . . . is a framework for doers—problem solvers, managers, policy makers, and policy analysts."[4] Precise definition may not be essential to the concerned individual who writes a check to a food pantry or serves meals at the homeless shelter, for that person in all likelihood acts more on the basis of some visceral rather than analytical understanding of the nature of the problem. For the helping individual, the definitional fine points—say, the distinction between hunger and malnutrition—are largely irrelevant. But for the purposes of crafting a collective policy response to hunger, a more systematic understanding is the first order of business. Definition implies a choice, a particular way of seeing a problem among a range of alternatives. Policy is determined in part by that choice, because the response, say to the malnourished (an early definition of hunger), is likely to be quite different from the response to those who present no symptoms of malnutrition but nevertheless do not enjoy "food security" (another definition). In short, as Roger Cobb and Charles Elder write, "To define a policy problem is to imply its solution and to delimit its solution possibilities."[5]

Definition serves yet another policy function: it helps to target and thus conserve resources. Definition provides nuance: a good definition may help, for example, to distinguish those in desperate crisis from those simply at risk of hunger. A definition thus increases the probability that resources will be spent efficiently.

Defining Hunger in the American Context

Over the past three decades or so, political leaders, policy analysts, nutritionists, advocates for the hungry, and others have proposed a bewildering variety of definitions. From one perspective this struggle over definitions simply reflects the difficulty of developing precise, useful terminology to describe a state of serious discomfort and deprivation that often fails to exhibit clear medical symptoms. The problem is compounded by the fact that almost everyone at some time experiences hunger—that sensation we may casually describe when dinner is late or a meal is skipped. But most would agree that this mild discomfort constitutes neither a social nor a medical problem and is hardly a suitable object of public policy. Yet where is the conceptual dividing line between "hunger" and "Hunger"?

From another perspective, the disagreement over definition is the product of competing professional and political agendas. For example, even though a consensus has finally emerged among most interested participants in the hunger policy community on the use of the term "food insecurity" to describe food deprivation in the United States, differences regarding its key descriptors remain. "Food insecurity" was meant to take the focus beyond nutritional issues, but most nutritionists still include a reference to the intake of "nutritionally adequate" food in the definition.[6] Some of those particularly active as policy advocates are also concerned that the term "food insecurity," which undeniably represents a conceptual advance, simply does not resonate as powerfully in the political world as the word "hunger."[7]

From yet a third perspective, the problem of defining hunger reflects the effort to craft a definition of the problem that fits the American context, where hunger must be understood not in the context of scarcity but rather in one of consistent and widely available abundance.[8]

The story of definition and the inextricably linked problem of measurement that unfolds in this and the next chapter is not a simple one. Initial efforts to define hunger assumed that it could be understood through a medical framework as a problem of malnutrition. Gradually this view gave way to a sociological understanding of food deprivation that seemed to describe the American case of food deprivation in a more accurate and useful way. The sociological perspective rejects both the third world framework of scarcity and medical standards of judgment by portraying hunger as a result of severe "food insecurity," a problem of limited access to adequate food in an abundant society.[9] Food insecurity provided a more nuanced understanding of levels of food deprivation. As a consensus formed on the superiority of the concept of food insecurity, many analysts seemed to treat the term as synonomous with hunger. In recent years, however, food insecurity has come to mean a condition of being at risk of hunger. Thus what began to emerge in the late 1990s is an understanding of the hunger problem as a continuum with points ranging from food insecurity without the sensation of hunger to severe hunger. Operational indicators for the points on the continuum are still a matter of debate.

Hunger as Malnutrition

Hunger became a truly public issue in the United States only in the late 1960s, even though a number of major federal food assistance programs were already in place. The crucial period during which the issue emerged was bracketed by the April 1967 visit to the Mississippi Delta by the Senate Subcommittee on Employment, Manpower, and Poverty, led by Joseph Clark (D-Pa.) and Robert Kennedy (D-N.Y.), and the broadcast on May 21, 1968, of the CBS television documentary, "Hunger in America."[10]

The initial impulse in defining hunger was to take what we knew about African or Asian or Latin American hunger and apply it to the domestic situation. In his opening remarks at the first set of Senate hearings in 1967 after the famous trip to the Mississippi Delta, Senator Clark noted that "Senator Kennedy of New York observed that the conditions we saw in the delta were as bad as any he had seen in his extensive tour of South America. One of the doctors who will testify today, and who has had extensive experience in Africa, has said that conditions he observed in this country are as bad or worse than those in Kenya and Aden."[11] Hunger abroad was associated with death and disease, and there was no reason at first to suppose that domestic hunger was any different. Moreover, the discovery of disease and other severe manifestations in Mississippi provided confirmation of what was otherwise almost unbelievable.[12] It was common, therefore, in this initial period of awareness to portray hunger as an extreme physiological condition.

The assumption that American and third world hunger ought to be understood in terms of the same critical physiological conditions underlay the methodology of a report on hunger released in the spring of 1968 by a private group that had constituted itself as the Citizens' Board of Inquiry into Hunger and Malnutrition in the United States. The report, *Hunger, U.S.A.*, used high postneonatal mortality rates as an indicator of the existence of hunger, and on this basis identified 280 "hunger counties" across the country.[13]

A similar perspective informed much of the CBS television documentary on hunger, aired a month later. In one segment of the film the reporter visits a Navajo reservation in Arizona and interviews a Public Health Service doctor. The following exchange takes place:

Dr. Van Duzen: Let me show you one of the real kwashiorkors.
Reporter: This child is representative of the sort of thing you find here?
Dr. Van Duzen: He still shows some of the signs of kwashiorkor.
Reporter: What is—you keep using that word "kwashiorkor." What is it?
Dr. Van Duzen: Kwashiorkor is the most severe form of protein calorie malnutrition. This is a disease that was first seen in South America and Africa. It's not supposed to exist in the United States, but it does. . . . I've seen about four cases a year . . . and I've seen other cases, so there's a lot of it.[14]

In an earlier segment the reporter travels to a San Antonio clinic, whose director of social services claims that nearly all of the 300 patients seen each day are suffering from malnutrition. Many of the adults look ten or twenty years older than they really are, and the malnourished children suffer chronic and occasionally fatal diarrhea, she reports. Later the scene of the documentary shifts to Alabama cotton country, where a different reporter notes that "slow starvation has become part of the Southern way of life."[15]

On the heels of the release of the Citizens' Board report and the broadcast of "Hunger in America," both houses of Congress initiated hearings "to investigate the extent of hunger and malnutrition" in the United States. As a result of its initial investigation, the Senate Subcommittee on Employment, Manpower, and Poverty decided to establish a Senate Select Committee on Nutrition and Human Needs, and it held further hearings at the beginning of the winter. What is interesting about these investigations from a definitional standpoint is the consistency with which members of Congress as well as those who testified in these hearings routinely link the terms "hunger" and "malnutrition." The former cannot be separated from the latter; they are parts of the same problem. Senator Winston Prouty (R-Vt.) speaks of the "problem of malnutrition and hunger," and his use of the singular ("problem") to refer to both hunger and malnutrition is common in this period. Senator Gaylord Nelson (D-Wis.) notes that "there is no doubt that hunger and malnutrition exists [*sic*] in this country," and he goes on to list their manifestations, including obesity induced by excess starches and inadequate protein, loss of muscle tone, distended stomachs, rickets, and various skin diseases.[16] In subsequent hearings a Cornell University professor of nutrition uses the same phrase, "hunger and malnutrition," later explaining that the terms "hunger," "starvation," and "malnutrition" "have no clear boundaries and no clear dividing lines."[17]

In its interim report a year later the Senate select committee admits that "much confusion has surrounded the terms 'hunger,' 'starvation,' and 'malnutrition'. . . . Hunger is . . . used, often interchangeably with 'undernutrition' or 'malnutrition.'"[18] This report too uses the terms together, as it summarizes a variety of field studies and interviews to document the extent of malnutrition in the United States and its effects on child development and health.

Equating hunger with malnutrition and other pathologies began to break down, however, within a few years of this initial period of discovery of the problem. By 1969 White House conferees meeting on food and nutrition issues took care to distinguish hunger from more serious consequences of food deprivation.

> Hunger is a biologic phenomenon and is not in itself indicative
> of disease or of unsatisfactory nutritional status. It should be
> clearly distinguished from undernutrition (chronic calorie defi-
> ciency) and malnutrition (disease caused by deficiency, excess or
> imbalance of nutrients). . . . Persistent hunger . . . is likely to
> precede undernutrition and should be alleviated in the absence
> of disease.[19]

Several years later the Senate Select Committee on Nutrition and Human Needs published a study of the distribution of hunger by county that further divorced the definition of hunger from pathological markers. Part of the intent was to report on the status of the 280 "hunger counties" identified in 1968 by the Citizens' Board of Inquiry. But whereas the earlier study had used postneonatal mortality rates as a key indicator of the existence of hunger, the new investigation used poverty levels. Staff researchers explicitly rejected the use of postneonatal mortality rates to designate hunger counties: data on infant deaths simply confuse the issue, the investigators contended, for survival depends "on both the adequacy of

the diet *and the general availability of medical care.*"[20] Poverty levels in each
county served as a better indicator of hunger, they said. Even though
people below the official federal poverty line theoretically cannot buy the
minimally adequate diet designated by USDA as the Economy Food Plan,
and thus are "by definition . . . improperly nourished," the focus of the
committee in 1973 was not the hungry individual's health condition but
his or her peripheral economic status in a well-off society.[21]

Although some people persisted through the 1970s in coupling hunger
and malnutrition, particularly those who had been among the first to call
attention to the problem, a more fully articulated sociological definition
was clearly emerging.[22] Researchers at USDA introduced the idea of
"potential hunger" in a 1980 report entitled *Progress Toward Eliminating
Hunger in America*. People could be said to suffer "potential hunger" if they
lacked resources to purchase food, lacked access to food distribution outlets or production resources, or lacked knowledge regarding how to find
and/or how to select food.[23] Again, sociological considerations—poverty
and social isolation or marginality—and not disease symptoms were
emerging as keys to identifying the hungry.

Food Sufficiency and Food Security

In its 1977–78 national food consumption survey USDA began to ask
whether people thought they got enough to eat all of the time. The question was worded as follows:

> Which of the following statements best describes the food eaten
> in your household:
> 1. Enough and the kinds of food we want to eat,
> 2. Enough but not always what we want to eat,
> 3. Sometimes not enough to eat, or
> 4. Often not enough to eat?

Although the question did not represent a deliberate effort either to influence the definitional debate over the nature of hunger or to measure its
incidence, it had an obvious practical and intuitive appeal. Some version of
the food insufficiency question came eventually to be incorporated in most
subsequent surveys devoted to exploring the scope of hunger in the United
States.

Participants in the intellectual struggle over the proper definition of hunger also found the simple food sufficiency question useful, but in itself inadequate. As Sheldon Margen of the Berkeley School of Public Health pointed out, the effort "to define hunger as the existence of individual or household food shortages or the actual perception of 'being hungry' . . . still misses many people who have to scavenge for food or depend on emergency food sources. While these people may avoid feeling hungry, they certainly have serious hunger problems."[24] Nevertheless, despite its problems, the notion of sufficiency or adequacy became one of the key elements in the sociological definition of hunger as the absence of "food security."

Sufficiency and the companion idea of ready and regular access to food supplies appear together in the effort by a group of officials in the Department of Health, Education, and Welfare to articulate hunger and nutrition policy goals in the wake of the 1969 White House food conference. Eventually this group organized a nutrition coordinating committee, which drafted a national nutrition policy statement. "All citizens," the statement read, "shall have access to an adequate and safe supply of food and ability to identify, select, and prepare an optimal diet, irrespective of social or economic status."[25]

The elaboration of a sociological definition gradually emerged in official government documents and through the efforts by people in the academic and hunger policy communities. The *Report of the President's Task Force on Food Assistance* (1984), for example, offers a distinction between a clinical definition of hunger ("relatively easy to quantify" by gauging the rate of underweight among children and the incidence of other nutritional deficiencies) and the commonsense definition, "a situation in which someone cannot obtain an adequate amount of food, even if the shortage is not prolonged enough to cause health problems."[26] This latter condition "bespeaks the existence of a social, not a medical, problem."[27] The report arrives at the obvious conclusion that there is "evidence of hunger [when] some people have difficulty obtaining adequate access to food."[28]

Simultaneously, a number of academic nutritionists were arriving at a similar understanding that food security inhered in ready access to adequate food.[29] This bore a close resemblance to parallel efforts at the international level to think about food security, a condition defined by the United Nations Food and Agriculture Organization in 1983 as a situation in which "all people at all times have both physical and economic access to the basic food they need."[30] For their own society, however, Americans added the requirement that access had to be through conventional food supply channels, such as grocery stores, co-ops, gardens, and restaurants, as opposed to unconventional food sources, such as soup kitchens, food pantries, and scavenging.

The idea of access to normal food sources offers the critical link to understanding the problem of hunger in an affluent society. As Margen has argued, "The use of abnormal or emergency food channels is considered an indicator of hunger since food is abundant in our country and only those with food security (hunger) problems will have to depend on these sources for food."[31] Thus the conceptualization of hunger as a problem of food insecurity is most useful in the context of a society in which the norm is the existence of a dense, stable network of well-endowed sources of food to which nearly all people assume regular, ready access. Obviously, a definition of hunger that relies on the notion of individual access to abundantly stocked "normal" food channels is inappropriate for societies that experience famine or whose food stocks fluctuate significantly over time.

By the beginning of the 1990s food insecurity had emerged as the preferred framework for understanding American hunger, not only in the advocacy community, but also in the policymaking world.[32] In a brief report designed to summarize the state of knowledge about domestic hunger, the House select committee embraces the concept of food security as an alternative to "malnutrition-focused efforts in the Third World."[33] The report cites testimony to the effect that reliance on a malnutrition standard inevitably misses the hungry who do not yet exhibit signs of physical pathology, yet nevertheless experience physical discomfort and distress. Hunger from this perspective is "subclinical."[34]

Yet if a general consensus had formed on the concept of food security, there nevertheless were—and still are—many competing specific definitions of the term. Definitional variations can be frustrating to the extent that they hinder the development of common empirical indicators and scales to measure food insecurity. But agreement on a common theme— lack of reliable access to sufficient food through the normal channels of food acquisition—represents a genuine advance in the conceptualization of hunger, or better, the hunger problem: the notion of food security has allowed the hunger policy community to cast the definitional net beyond physiological boundaries. The idea of food insecurity makes clear that the inability to obtain abundant food supplies may have a range of social and psychological as well as physical consequences, including dependency on emergency food sources, resort to theft, family breakdown, anxiety, depression, and poor school performance.[35] Thus the use of the concept of food security—which the House select committee had begun to assert as a "fundamental right"—has broad policy implications, for it suggests that solutions extend beyond the mere provision of food to address the barriers to access to abundance, such as poverty.[36]

Definition and the Culture of Abundance

The struggle to define hunger is a story about coming to terms with a kind of human deprivation in the midst of an abundant society. This has been no easy task. Initial definitions were developed without reference to the cultural context of a distinctive American nexus of economic affluence, overwhelming agricultural capacity, and the presumption of plenty. Progress occurred only when analysts began to think of the problem as a lack of access to a more than ample abundance, a particularly American problem.

This chapter has recounted the evolution of a hunger definition both as an intellectual construct and as an increasingly useful guide to policy. The rejection of a narrow clinical definition meant that hunger policies could move beyond nutrition issues to address problems as diverse as the sources of poverty, the skewed geographical distribution of retail food outlets, and the shortcomings of private food assistance.

The achievement of a consensus on hunger as a problem mainly of food insecurity raises new issues, however. In the world of politics, "food insecurity," compared with the word "hunger," has a certain bloodless ring to it. It is hard to imagine that "food insecurity" elicits much emotional or political resonance among either public officials or the citizenry. Thus if policy scholars and analysts have managed to make progress in understanding hunger, there clearly remain issues in the larger political world between those who would seek to mobilize public concern and those who seek to define.

3 | *Measuring Hunger in the United States*

As Americans began to understand that hunger was a chronic condition for sizable numbers of people, government and nonprofit organizations embarked on efforts to measure its prevalence. Since the late 1960s substantial resources have been devoted to this task, producing a welter of data on nutrition, food consumption patterns, demand for emergency food service, childhood and elderly hunger, and food insecurity. Literally hundreds of studies have been undertaken. Most of these have explored hunger at the state or local level; a few have attempted to develop national estimates. Yet it took nearly three decades of effort before analysts could begin to say with precision how many Americans are hungry, who exactly they are, the intensity of their need, and the length of time they suffer.

Until the 1995 Current Population Survey, there had been no official attempt to achieve a hunger count, nor for most of this period had there been any single government agency with the responsibility for mounting a periodic hunger census. But problems have also hindered the collection of reliable data. Thus during the decades in which the major food assistance programs were being put in place, estimates by government and nongovernmental organizations of the national prevalence of hunger nationwide varied widely.

The difficulty of measuring hunger is tied first to the struggle to define hunger conceptually and then to the problem of agreeing on appropriate measurement indicators. As Kathy Radimer and her colleagues observed during the peak of this effort, "The current status of hunger assessment can be described as follows: hunger definitions vary widely, measures of hunger are generally indirect, direct measures are uncommon, and definitions and measures may lack congruence."[1]

Those who believed that hunger was indicated by malnutrition argued for national nutrition surveys. Others, who were convinced that hunger was less a physical than a social condition, sought instead to develop a checklist of behavioral and subjective indicators. But even as consensus emerged on the validity of a sociological definition of hunger, analysts continued to debate the best measures by which to gauge a subjective condition that cannot generally be observed directly.

What is striking to the policy historian is how long this debate lasted and how slowly the federal government responded. The first calls for measuring the extent of American hunger appeared at the very moment of its emergence in the public consciousness. The private citizens who constituted themselves a Citizens' Board of Inquiry into Hunger and Malnutrition and visited Mississippi and Appalachia in 1967 acknowledged that there was no definitive estimate of hunger in the United States, but they expressed the hope that such data would soon be collected by the federal government.[2] And witnesses in congressional hearings in those early years frequently commented on the lack of information, suggesting directly or implicitly that the situation be remedied. "We do not know the dimensions of the problem of hunger and malnutrition in the United States," Dr. Michael Latham told the Senate Select Committee on Nutrition and Human Needs in 1968. "Although the United States has conducted detailed nutrition surveys in many developing countries in four continents, there has been no comparable survey carried out in the United States."[3]

But these early concerns went essentially unheeded. Seventeen years after the famous visit by a team of senators and doctors to the Mississippi Delta,[4] President Reagan's Task Force on Food Assistance could still observe that "there is no official 'hunger count' to estimate the number of hungry people, and so there are no hard data available to estimate the extent of hunger directly. Those who argue that hunger is widespread and growing rely on indirect measures."[5] Nor had matters changed appreciably nearly a decade later. In a 1992 letter to the House select committee, J. Larry Brown, director of the Tufts University Center on Hunger, Poverty and Nutrition Policy, asserted that "sufficient data to provide a single definitive estimate of the dimensions of hunger do not exist. . . . Neither the Census Bureau nor other agencies monitor the incidence of hunger within the population."[6]

Measurement Issues

Without consensus on a definition of hunger, analysts had to choose from among a number of options in attempting to measure its prevalence. Four basic measurement strategies have been employed for estimating the scope of hunger: the use of medical and dietary data, tied to the idea that hunger is best understood in terms of malnutrition; the resort to a poverty proxy; the analysis of demand for food assistance; and the collection of survey data on perceived food sufficiency, anxiety, eating patterns, and coping behaviors, efforts informed to one degree or another by the notion of food insecurity. These strategies are best explored in the context of actual measurement efforts, but it is useful at the outset to understand their fundamental features, both positive and negative.

For those who have defined hunger in terms of malnutrition, examining the health status of populations thought to be at particular risk is an obvious choice. The advantage of this strategy is that there are well-accepted measurements of malnutrition.[7] Limiting measurement to at-risk groups—the poor, the unemployed, welfare recipients—focuses what might otherwise be an extremely costly undertaking. But the disadvantages are legion. As we have seen, most analysts have come to understand hunger as a condition that generally precedes malnutrition. In addition, conducting the necessary biochemical examinations among a sufficient sample of the population—even the high-risk population—is expensive and time-consuming.

Much early discussion of the scope of the problem by hunger analysts looked to data collected by the federal government not on malnutrition per se but on dietary deficiency. The latter is a necessary precondition of the former, but dietary deficiency may not lead to malnutrition or even to the sensations of discomfort or distress that we associate with hunger. Thus using data on dietary deficiency to gauge the prevalence of hunger is a stretch, for it has never been clear at what precise point nutritional deficiency shades into hunger.

A second strategy for measuring hunger has been to assume that anyone below the official federal poverty line is probably hungry. The prevalence of hunger, then, is some function of the prevalence of poverty. The logic of this simple measure is that the poverty line is based on having sufficient income to spend on USDA's minimally adequate diet. An income below the poverty line means that personal or family food expenditures likely fall short of the necessary minimum.

Poverty is, however, a highly imperfect proxy for hunger. Many poor people are able to feed themselves adequately, as the 1995 CPS data show.[8] Other data support this finding. For example, a national nutrition survey found that even among those whose incomes fell below the official poverty line, 84.1 percent reported that they get enough food to eat.[9] A study of low-income households in Allegheny County, Pennsylvania, found that of those below the federal poverty line, only 22 percent met the necessary criteria to be classified as "food insecure."[10]

Conversely, some people with incomes above the poverty line are unable to spend enough to maintain a minimally adequate diet. Beth Osborne Daponte's study of Allegheny County low-income households found that more than one-third of her sample whose incomes lay above the poverty line by as much 185 percent nevertheless could be deemed "food insecure."[11] High housing or medical costs may reduce the portion of income normally set aside for food. If such people cannot supplement their food purchases with public or private food assistance, they may suffer some level of food insecurity but not be counted as such by using the poverty line indicator.

A third common method for gauging hunger is through an analysis of patterns of demand for help. Trends in the number of people seeking federal food assistance or visits to food pantries and soup kitchens are commonly used to draw inferences about the dimensions of hunger. These indirect measures raise all sorts of questions. Some analysts have cautioned, for example, that growing use of food pantries may reflect an increase in the availability of humanitarian aid rather than an increase in hunger. According to President Reagan's Task Force on Food Assistance, "The amount of food which the private sector makes available has increased independently of the growth of the population in need."[12] Data on demand levels also do not reveal what proportion of hungry people avail themselves of food assistance. Federal food aid programs collect data on the proportion of eligibles who participate, but this is not the same as the proportion of hungry. Private food charities rarely make a claim that they know the extent of their coverage of the hungry population. It is also sometimes difficult in using demand data to distinguish the number of visits to a food assistance facility from the number of individual visitors: some clients may be frequent users while others appear only occasionally.[13] Rising demand on food assistance programs or services may thus be a function of increasing numbers of hungry people or it may be that the same number of hungry people are using food assistance more frequently.

The fourth method of gathering data on the prevalence of hunger is through surveys, either of random samples of the population at large or of targeted subsets of the population, such as children, the poor, or the elderly. Surveying for this purpose is not a simple matter. Hunger may affect members of the same household in different ways: for example, a parent will often forgo food to feed a child. Thus it is useful in a survey to distinguish household from individual hunger and to explore the different degrees of deprivation among members of the household.[14] Hunger may also be experienced chronically (say, the last week of the month when food stamps run out) or sporadically; capturing the time dimension is also important.

Survey instruments can capture different aspects of food insecurity as experienced by households and individuals: insufficient quantity of food, limited or inadequate quality of food, food anxiety (fear that one's food supply will not last or a sense of deprivation), and a social component that includes obtaining food from unconventional sources, such as begging or scavenging, or coping behaviors, such as skipping meals.[15]

Early Measurement Efforts

Modern attempts to establish the national prevalence of hunger fall into two periods. The first lasted just over a decade, extending from the Citizens' Board of Inquiry report in 1968 to a set of hearings in the Senate Subcommittee on Nutrition in 1979 that included testimony by the original Field Foundation team of doctors who had visited the South in 1967. The second period stretches from the early Reagan years to the present. The first period is dominated by the effort to wrest a hunger count from data on the nutrition and poverty status of the American population. Measurement efforts in the more recent period have largely been informed by the idea of food sufficiency and the development of the concept of food security. In the early period, as chapter 2 has shown, hunger was scarcely understood except in the context of malnutrition. "Hunger" and "malnutrition" were terms used in tandem. In retrospect the focus on malnutrition seems not simply a matter of theoretical conviction but also a matter of expedience. In 1989 Senate hearings on the history of hunger measurement efforts, Cheryl Wehler of the Community Childhood Hunger Identification Project observed that "hunger surveys in the United States have their origin in nutrition surveys."[16] She went on to explain that hunger was historically defined in terms of its nutritional consequences in order to facilitate the measurement of what was a subjective state. Clinical, anthropometric, and biochemical data would presumably provide the hard evidence from which to draw conclusions about the incidence of hunger.[17]

This was the assumption of the Citizens' Board of Inquiry, whose members had visited several poverty-stricken regions of the United States in 1967 and 1968. Each team included at least one physician and/or nutritionist. Although the principal data-gathering technique involved hearings at which hungry people and emergency food providers testified, the teams also reviewed studies and gathered testimony and data on clinical malnutrition from local doctors and hospitals.[18] The board concluded in its report, "We have found concrete evidence of chronic hunger and malnutrition in every part of the United States where we have held hearings or conducted field trips."[19]

But what was the prevalence of "hunger and malnutrition" in national terms? The board admitted that "no definitive estimate can now be made regarding the number of people who suffer from hunger and malnutrition in the United States," but it went on nevertheless to offer a figure of 10 million people.[20]

Shortly after the Citizens' Board of Inquiry offered its estimate, Senator George McGovern's (D-S.D.) Senate Select Committee on Nutrition and Human Needs, newly created to investigate hunger issues, declared that there could be as many as 14.4 million hungry people in the United States.[21] The claim is a confusing one, however. The 14.4 million are alternately called "victims of poverty-related hunger and malnutrition" and "Americans who are so poor that they must have assistance if they are to escape malnutrition."[22] The select committee arrived at its estimate by adding the 5.1 million "very poor" (those whose total incomes fell below the cost of the USDA Economy Food Plan, the cost of which is multiplied by three to arrive at the federal poverty line) to the 9.3 million whose incomes totaled only between one and two times the cost of the Economy Food Plan. These two groups are so poor that they could not in all likelihood afford to purchase even this minimal diet. It is not clear, however, why the select committee decided not to include among the likely hungry the remaining 10.6 million people officially classified as poor. Their incomes, after all, fell between two and three times the cost of the Economy Food Plan. Any income below three times the cost (the poverty line) arguably threatens a family's ability to buy the full minimal diet. The select committee did note that this slightly better-off group, while "not certain to be suffering from malnutrition, probably suffer[s] from periods of nutritional deficiency and . . . [is] continually at risk."[23]

Still focused on equating hunger with malnutrition, the select committee admitted that it could not say precisely whether even the 14.4 million figure provided an accurate hunger count without additional study to determine the "extent and severity of clinically and biochemically validated malnutrition."[24] It further qualified its estimate by noting that the 14.4 million people could be counted among the hungry *unless they are receiving food assistance.*"[25] Since by the committee's calculations slightly less than half the 14.4 million received food stamps or participated in the federal commodity distribution program, this meant that the hunger count was reduced to about 8 million. All in all, the Senate select committee's calculations did little to clarify the issue of the scope of hunger.

All expectations were that a more definitive estimate of the prevalence of hunger and malnutrition was on the way. In the Partnership for Health Amendment of 1967, Congress had directed the secretary of the Department of Health, Education, and Welfare to "make a comprehensive survey of the incidence and location of serious hunger and malnutrition and health problems incident thereto in the United States." The task was assigned to the Nutrition Program in the Public Health Service. An ad hoc advisory committee appointed to assist in the design of the survey quickly decided that a national undertaking was too costly and recommended a more limited study. Eventually, ten states were selected for what came to be called the Ten-State Nutrition Survey.[26]

The survey represented the most comprehensive effort of its kind ever undertaken: dietary data were gathered through interviews of representatives of 24,000 low-income families (86,000 individuals); nearly half the families also participated in clinical tests. Yet when the General Accounting Office, at McGovern's request, reviewed the study several years after it was published, it concluded that the survey had "failed to comply with the intent of Congress." Investigators had not been able to gather data that "would permit meaningful examination of the relationship between hunger and poverty except in the crudest terms."[27]

The Ten-State Nutrition Survey fell short of expectations because it was plagued from the beginning by delays, funding cuts, and controversy. When the study director reported preliminary findings from Texas and Louisiana that between one-third and one-half of all those surveyed exhibited anemia or other critical nutritional deficiencies, the survey was removed from his control and relocated to the Centers for Disease Control and Prevention (then known as the Communicable Disease Center) in Atlanta.[28] When the final five-volume report was finally published, years late, it was clear that it had failed to provide an estimate of the national prevalence of hunger.[29] The results of the clinical examinations turned up little evidence of "severe nutritional deficiencies" (though the report warned that malnutrition had to be of long duration to produce obvious clinical signs).[30] Hunger as a subjective state or a problem of inadequate food intake is never mentioned in the final five-volume report. And by the study director's own testimony, data on food consumption, based on the respondent's recall of the family's dietary intake for the prior twenty-four-hour period, were inadequate to establish reliable information on long-term patterns of eating or deprivation.[31]

By the end of the 1970s the federal government was no closer than it had been a decade earlier to establishing a reliable hunger count. McGovern, now the chair of the Senate Subcommittee on Nutrition of the Agriculture Committee and a major figure in the development of food assistance policy, sought to take stock. He called a hearing at which the senators heard testimony from a group of doctors who in 1977 had revisited the same areas of the South and Appalachia in search of malnutrition that they had toured in 1967. The doctors testified that a decade of federal food programs had, according to their observations, greatly reduced the number of "grossly malnourished" people over the course of the decade. But when McGovern pressed a witness to provide an estimate of the number of hungry people in the United States, the doctor was unable to offer one.[32]

In retrospect, the failure of government and other analysts to measure the prevalence of hunger in this early period is understandable: both the poverty proxy and malnutrition approaches were simply too oblique to tell us much about the American hunger problem. These easily measurable though indirect indicators were derived by reference to what we knew about hunger in foreign countries, not its domestic variant. As one health official commented in hearings in 1989, "Nutrition data do not currently have the capability to evaluate the relationship of nutritional status to food security."[33] Poverty and malnutrition, then, were extremely blunt and misleading indicators. But no theory of hunger yet provided a sharper focus.

A More Complex View of Hunger Prevalence

Even as the Senate select committee was seeking unsuccessfully to take a national hunger count, USDA was preparing to report national findings from its 1977–78 food consumption survey on self-reported perceptions of household food sufficiency. USDA has been collecting general information on the food consumption habits of Americans since the 1890s; regular national sample surveys date from the 1930s. The objectives of the food consumption surveys have never included the determination of the prevalence of hunger. Instead, the purposes of the survey, conducted approximately once a decade, have been to assist Congress and other federal agencies in developing and administering programs relating to food production and marketing, to help the food industry to adjust production and processing to conform to consumer demand, and to permit nutritionists to gauge the nutritive value of the American diet.[34] Hunger, the maldistribution of foodstuffs, deprivation, and even malnutrition are not mentioned as concerns.

Until the publication of the 1977–78 data, analysts combing the earlier surveys for clues to the incidence of hunger had to rely on data on the number of households in which diets provided less than the recommended daily allowance of various nutrients. Thus, for example, Judith Segal reproduces data from the 1965–66 survey showing that 9 million low-income households had diets that could be classified as deficient by some standard.[35] Although the problem of dietary deficiency was concentrated disproportionately among the low-income population, the data also showed that 20 percent of all American households, including many with middle-class incomes, had diets that provided less than two-thirds of the recommended allowance for at least one nutrient.[36] It was impossible to draw useful conclusions about the prevalence of hunger from these data.

Revised Household Food Consumption Surveys

But in the 1977–78 survey, USDA included for the first time its food sufficiency question (see chapter 2). Exactly why the agency suddenly decided to ask people if they normally had enough to eat is not clear. A member of the federal interagency group that devised the questionnaire does not recall that there was any sense that USDA was breaking new ground in the study of hunger or food deprivation, even though she agreed that in retrospect the question was a departure from the malnutrition framework that still dominated the understanding of hunger.[37] It is likely that USDA, in devising the question, was not thinking about hunger at all, for the mission of the food consumption survey has nothing to do with determining a hunger count. The results of the food sufficiency question are not discussed at all in the text of the multivolume report of the 1977–78 survey, which suggests the lack of significance USDA analysts accorded the question. The data are reported only as a small part of one of the hundreds of tables.[38]

Yet the question has since assumed much greater significance. It has been included in every subsequent national and supplemental USDA food consumption survey, providing a useful longitudinal view. In addition, with modest variations in wording it has become a standard element in the batteries of questions asked in other surveys by both private and government investigators who seek to measure food security. The question serves as a bridge from the early period of measurement efforts, during which hunger was equated with malnutrition, to the more recent period in which hunger is understood more broadly as a problem of food insecurity.

The 1977–78 question is intended to measure the respondent's perception of the adequacy of the household food supply. In itself the question says nothing about a person's food or nutrient intake. It does not ask anything about feelings of hunger, sources of food, how people cope with insufficiency, or food expenditures. It does not specify a time frame, making it impossible to tell whether insufficiency is long- or short-term. In the USDA household food consumption survey the question is asked only of individuals in households in the continental forty-eight states; the survey does not include Alaskans or Hawaiians, nor does it cover the homeless or people in institutions. USDA thus insists that its use of this single question cannot provide a measure of hunger for the population as a whole.[39] Nevertheless, USDA researchers have also written that "when respondents indicate the insufficiency of household food supplies, it is reasonable to expect that these households are experiencing 'hunger,' since at least some household members are not getting enough to eat."[40]

Subsequent research based on a secondary analysis of the food consumption survey data has demonstrated that those respondents who say

Table 3-1. *Perceptions of Food Inadequacy, Selected Years, 1977–91*
Percent of respondents[a]

Year	Low income[b]	All income levels
1977–78	12.5	3.0
1979–80[c]	14.9	n.a.
1985[d]	14.3	3.6
1986[d]	16.0	3.7
1987–88	11.3	3.4
1989[e]	7.7	2.1
1990	10.7	2.6
1991	11.0	3.0

Source: Unpublished data from the Nationwide Food Consumption Surveys, 1977–91 (Department of Agriculture, Human Nutrition Information Service, 1995).

n.a. Not available.

a. Respondents indicated that they "sometimes" or "often" do not have enough to eat.

b. Incomes less than or equal to 130 percent of the federal poverty line.

c. A supplemental survey of low-income households only.

d. Surveys were limited to households with at least one woman between the ages of 19 and 50.

e. Department of Agriculture warns that because of the small sample size for 1989–91, as well as the new weighting procedures, the numbers are entirely preliminary and require additional investigation.

that there is sometimes or often not enough food in their household in fact have significantly lower levels of food spending and food and nutrient intakes than those who say they always have enough food.[41] Intake was calculated from a twenty-four-hour dietary recall of the day prior to the survey. In addition, among those who said there was not always enough to eat in their households, food expenditures were significantly lower. Thus although it still cannot be said that food insufficiency is a completely satisfactory indicator of hunger, the question offered a more informative way to count those experiencing food deprivation than anything prior to the USDA survey.

Data from food consumption surveys from 1977–78 through 1991 are presented in table 3-1. Several caveats are in order. Data for 1985 and 1986 are only for households with at least one woman between the ages of nineteen and fifty. In addition, beginning in 1989 the Human Nutrition Information Service changed the sample weighting procedure, which had the effect, in all likelihood, of reducing the percentages in those years. USDA was not sufficiently confident in the figures from 1989 to 1991 to publish them officially. Nonetheless, viewed with caution, the data based on the food insufficiency question are suggestive.

Extrapolating to the national population is risky, since it is not clear that everyone in each household with insufficient food experiences hunger. Parents may go hungry, for example, in order to feed their children. Furthermore, as noted above, the survey does not cover certain population groups, including the homeless.[42] The inability particularly to derive reliable individual hunger estimates from household food insufficiency data constitutes a major weakness of the Household Food Consumption Survey question as an indicator of hunger prevalence. Nevertheless, assuming for a moment that all members of households with insufficient food do experience hunger at some time, the food insufficiency question yields a total number of hungry people living in households (that is, who are neither homeless nor in institutions) at between 6.1 and 8.6 million, depending on the year.[43] These numbers are in the same vicinity as the estimates offered by the Senate select committee in 1969 and the Citizens' Board of Inquiry a year earlier.

Studies of Demand for Emergency Food Assistance

The transition in the hunger policy arena from the period dominated by the malnutrition framework to the later concern with food sufficiency and security coincided more or less with the administration of Jimmy Carter. Once Congress eliminated the purchase requirement for food stamps in 1977, the issue of hunger seems largely to have receded from the public consciousness. But matters changed with the recession of the early 1980s and the Reagan revolution. Between 1979 and 1983 the number of people below the poverty line rose by approximately 35 percent. At the same time the Reagan administration embarked on its effort to reduce federal domestic spending, engineering cuts, among other places, in many social welfare programs. Food stamps and the school breakfast and lunch programs were among those cut. Social service organizations and agencies in cities across the country began to report a surge in demand for emergency food assistance.

The network of mainly private food pantries, soup kitchens, and homeless shelters soon became the focus for a revived concern over the scope of hunger. Reports of the growth in the number of emergency food providers, client demand volume, and client characteristics proliferated. Although a few of these reports were national in scope, most were surveys of demand for assistance in particular states or communities.[44] Marion Nestle and Sally Gutmacher trace the growth in the number of such studies by date of issue: from three in 1981, the number grew to nineteen in 1982, thirty-one in 1983, and forty in 1984.[45]

Studies of demand for food assistance from street-level providers offer no basis for estimating the prevalence of hunger, either nationally or within any subnational jurisdiction. They rarely produce comparable results, making aggregation or meaningful cross-jurisdiction contrasts impossible. For example, in their review of fifty such hunger studies, the settings of which extend from Dade County, Florida, to the inner city of Cleveland to a rural multi-county area in northern Idaho, Barbara Cohen and Martha Burt find that among the client populations of emergency food pantries the proportion of families headed by a single parent ranges from 38 percent to 77 percent; elderly clients of food pantries comprise between 7 percent and 38 percent; and the proportion of clients with young children ranged from 52 percent to 80 percent.[46] The studies provide no basis for explaining these sharp variations.

Such investigations offer no way of estimating hunger (nor for the most part do they purport to), for there is no way of telling from these data what proportion of hungry people seek food assistance from charitable sources. Not only is it likely that some unknown number of hungry people never avail themselves of such emergency food services, but also some who might be inclined to seek help may live in places not served at all by such providers. At best, then, these studies can be used to document local changes in the burden on emergency food sources, changes in the number of providers, and the characteristics of the client population.

With these limitations in mind, at least two studies are nevertheless important to note, for they represent the broadest perspective on the growth of the emergency food assistance sector and its expanding client base. One is the continuing effort by the U.S. Conference of Mayors (USCM) to document the demand on emergency food providers in cities. The other is a national survey of food banks and their member agencies by Second Harvest, the largest private food charity in the United States.

USCM conducted its first survey in 1982, gathering information on public and private food providers in fifty-five cities. In the following decade the mayors' organization reported twenty-three more times on hunger and homelessness.[47] Reports now appear annually. Unfortunately, USCM did not use a panel format for its survey: each study is based on a different number of cities, selected nonrandomly. The principal criterion for a city's inclusion in that year's survey seems to be the mayor's membership on the USCM Task Force on Hunger and Homelessness. After surveying fifty-five cities in 1982, the USCM reported on only twenty cities in 1984, forty in 1985, twenty-five in 1986, twenty-seven in 1989, and twenty-nine in 1995.

The utility of these surveys is therefore limited, but what they do show is that each year in each study most of the cities report an increase in the demand on public and private agencies offering free food to the hungry. Prior to 1995, no fewer than 83 percent of the cities surveyed in any given year reported an increase in demand over the prior year on emergency food services.[48] Although the magnitude of increases varies widely from city to city, demand appears to be growing in all sizes of urban centers and in all parts of the country.

A more careful and more useful survey of emergency food providers was conducted in 1993 under the sponsorship of Second Harvest.[49] In its role as an umbrella organization for food banks around the country, Second Harvest surveyed both food service clients and affiliated agencies. Of its 41,587 affiliated agencies, 3,200 were surveyed. The final report estimates that emergency food providers in the vast Second Harvest network of food pantries, soup kitchens, homeless shelters, and other programs served nearly 26 million individual clients one or more times during 1993. Second Harvest points out that this represents 10.4 percent of the U.S. population, but the organization does not claim the figure as a national hunger count.[50] Nevertheless, the scope of the survey and the care of its design warrant confidence in the conclusion that demand for emergency food services is both heavy and widespread.

Food Sufficiency and Food Security Surveys

Surveys of demand at food pantries, though critical to understanding the dimensions of the emergency hunger relief effort, still do not provide data with which to estimate the national prevalence of hunger. Progress toward that end has come instead through several private and public sample surveys that have sought to measure perceived food sufficiency and food security.

Important groundwork was laid by the nonprofit Food Research and Action Center (FRAC). Alarmed by the 1982 USCM report on the growing demand for emergency relief, FRAC began planning a major survey to study hunger among children. Its pioneering effort, the Community Childhood Hunger Identification Project (CCHIP), produced a battery of questions on which subsequent federal surveys have relied heavily.[51] CCHIP researchers set out "to broaden the conceptualization of hunger, in a way that is most appropriate to the socioeconomic context of the United States."[52] Since primary malnutrition is relatively rare among American children, more sensitive measures of "hunger . . . as a distinct phenomenon in industrialized settings" with a "relatively high standard of living" had to be devised.[53]

The CCHIP instrument was eventually composed of eight questions designed to measure both food insufficiency and insecurity pertaining to the experience of the respondent and his or her household members over both the preceding year and month. For each time period the questions ask whether the household ever runs out of money to buy food; whether adults or children eat less, rely on a limited number of foods, or skip meals because there is not enough money; whether children say they are hungry because there is not enough food in the house; and whether children ever go to bed hungry.[54]

The initial CCHIP consisted of seven surveys in 1989–90 in different parts of the country, the subjects of which were families earning less than 185 percent of the poverty line.[55] Respondents from 32 percent of the combined samples of households answered in the affirmative to at least five out of the eight questions. These households, representing one out of every eight families with children under twelve, were deemed "hungry." An additional 40 percent answered affirmatively to between one and four of the questions, and they were classified as being "at risk" of hunger. Extrapolating these findings to the national population, FRAC estimated that 5.5 million children under age twelve were hungry. An additional 6 million children were at risk of hunger.

Aside from focusing attention on the scope of childhood hunger, the most important contribution of the CCHIP study for understanding the hunger problem was its battery of survey questions. These helped subsequent surveyors to devise question sequences that explored food insecurity as a multidimensional phenomenon (individual and household, levels of deprivation and modes of coping) in a temporal context (last month and last year). This constituted a far more complex view of hunger than any survey had provided heretofore.

Another important survey, the third National Health and Nutrition Examination Survey (NHANES III), was mounted by the National Center for Health Statistics at the Centers for Disease Control. The survey went into the field in waves beginning in 1988. Data collection continued into late 1994. This massive survey, the third in a series, was designed to assess national health and nutrition status.[56] Questions about food sufficiency constitute just one small part of the investigation. The survey involves interviews regarding dietary intake and eating patterns with approximately 40,000 people. The sample is drawn from the entire civilian, noninstitutionalized U.S. population.

NHANES III includes the Household Food Consumption Survey question of whether there is sometimes or often not enough food to eat in the household. Preliminary analysis of these data found frequencies consistent with the USDA surveys reported in table 3-1. In the NHANES III survey covering data gathered in the period 1988–91, 3.9 percent of the national sample said that there was sometimes or often not enough to eat in their households.[57] Among low-income respondents, the figure was 12.9 percent. Extrapolating to the population as a whole by using 1990 figures on the number of households in the nation (93.4 million) and the average size of households (2.62 persons), we derive a figure of about 9.5 million people who live in households in which one member told surveyors that they had insufficient food.

The Current Population Survey of 1995

The CPS study has its origins in the National Nutrition Monitoring and Related Research Act of 1990. In 1992 an interagency federal task force began planning the survey, building on the concept of food insecurity and the operational advances tested and refined in the CCHIP, NHANES III, and several local surveys.[58] Based on 45,000 household interviews, the 1995 survey is the most comprehensive national portrait of hunger and food insecurity to date. The study distinguishes among those suffering food insecurity without hunger, food insecurity with moderate hunger (a household where an adult is hungry), and food insecurity with severe hunger (where a child has experienced hunger). The battery of questions, which range from whether the respondent is worried that food will run out to whether a child in the household had ever not eaten for a whole day because there was no food, is planned as an annual part of the CPS.

The estimated number of people living in food-insecure households with either moderate or severe hunger—11.2 million people—is slightly higher than estimates based on the food insufficiency question in previous surveys. Those earlier surveys produced estimates that ranged up to 8.6 million people in households that did not have enough to eat. Both the CPS and earlier figures are valid totals, however, only if every member of the households surveyed experienced hunger, which has not been ascertained in any of the household surveys. The number of people in food-insecure households where no actual hunger is reported is estimated at about 23.5 million.

The CPS data provide a more detailed demographic portrait of food insecurity than has been available heretofore.[59] The data are reported as the proportions of persons with selected characteristics living in households in each food security category. They show that food insecurity prevalences are about twice as high among blacks and Hispanics as among whites, and about three times as high among female heads of households as among families with married couples. Food insecurity is higher in central cities (18.3 percent) than in rural areas (13.5 percent). It is predictably lowest in suburban areas, although 10.7 percent of people in metropolitan areas outside of central cities live in food-insecure households. Food insecurity is lowest among the elderly of all population subgroups (5.4 percent).

Conclusions

After nearly three decades of effort, hunger analysts have finally achieved consensus on a measurement protocol for estimating the national prevalence of hunger. To understand how important this survey is for the purposes of thinking about food assistance policy, consider that until the 1995 CPS, it was common, particularly among advocacy groups and within the House Select Committee on Hunger, to assert that the number of Americans suffering from hunger ranged as high as 30 million.[60] But now we have begun to understand not only that there are gradations of deprivation but also that the number of genuinely hungry is probably significantly lower. Good data are important; among other things, for example, the CPS figures may permit policymakers to calibrate the food stamp allotment more carefully, increasing stamps for enrolled households still suffering food insecurity and examining carefully the role of food stamps in households deemed food secure. In addition, good data are essential to establish a baseline measure to observe fluctuations over time and to help policy analysts gauge the impact of interventions and the effects of macroeconomic and social forces.

4 | *The Food Stamp Program*

A deep economic recession in the early part of the Ford administration drove average monthly food stamp participation sharply upward to what were at the time record levels. With nearly a third more people receiving food stamps in 1975 than in the previous year, about one in twelve Americans was relying on this form of food assistance. To opponents of food stamps, the program seemed clearly out of control. By the end of the century, they predicted, a quarter or perhaps even half the American population would be buying their food with vouchers.[1]

Despite subsequent liberalization of eligibility standards and another sharp economic downturn in the early 1980s, the fears of such massive dependency did not come to pass. Nevertheless, food stamps did and do constitute a large aid program by any accounting. With the exception of medicaid, no other form of direct public assistance reaches so many poor Americans in any given year. In the year before the massive welfare reforms of 1996, the average monthly participation stood at about 26.6 million people, or slightly more than 10 percent of the population, and the annual cost to the nation was approximately $24.6 billion.

The food stamp program is a relatively effective form of assistance: the program is concentrated among the most needy, it increases food consumption among the poor, it is available to virtually all eligibles, and it enhances good nutrition. The stamps also produce higher levels of spending on food than equivalent cash transfers. All things considered, the simple design and broad accessibility of food stamps put within the grasp of American society the means to banish domestic food insecurity.

The food stamp program has failed to do this, however. A significant number of working and nonworking poor, homeless people, and recipients of other forms of cash welfare assistance do not participate in the program. Most legal immigrants were actually barred from the program by the 1996 welfare reform, although in 1998 Congress restored the eligibility for food stamps for roughly a quarter of that population.[2] Even many people enrolled in the food stamp program find that the stamps do not go far enough: they still do not get enough to eat.

No program is immune to the need for improvements, and it is clear that modest changes in design and implementation could improve the performance of the food stamp program. But the failure of food stamps to eradicate food insecurity is less a function of design flaws than it is of a set of issues that derive from the ambivalence toward social welfare that Americans bring to virtually all public programs of aid to the needy. People say they wish to be generous to the genuinely destitute, but they often believe that large numbers who receive public assistance are simply lazy or are cheats. Such ambivalence suggests a certain underlying doubt that significant numbers of people are truly hungry. This nagging doubt has a corrosive effect on the food stamp program, and it is manifested in the following ways:

— The program has been burdened by contradictory objectives that were designed to broaden political support but compromised its welfare aims.

— It has been harried by charges of fraud and abuse that opponents have used to challenge its legitimacy.

— It has been marked by low participation rates that stem from failures to reach out to the eligible, from the stigma recipients are made to feel, and from the complex certification process to establish and maintain eligibility.

— Its level of assistance historically has been inadequate to provide genuine food security for all food stamp recipients.

The effect of these four problems has been to curtail the ability of the food stamp program to address food insecurity in an optimal way.

Building the Food Stamp Program

The story of the food stamp program can be told quickly, for it has been the subject of several thorough accounts.[3] Food stamps were originally employed in 1939 as an alternative to the commodity distribution program that had been in effect since 1932. Food stamps were initiated by the secretary of agriculture under the authority vested in him by section 32 of the Agricultural Adjustment Act amendments of 1935, which gave him broad discretion in using tariff revenues to encourage domestic consumption of surplus foods. In the event, the poor used their food stamps to purchase a much broader range of foods than those stockpiled by the Federal Surplus Commodities Corporation, but if the new program did not reduce surplus holdings, it nevertheless had other unforeseen virtues: it provided a more varied diet for the needy, and it was regarded as beneficial to grocery stores and wholesalers. Lasting only four years, until 1943, the first food stamp program ultimately attained a peak enrollment of 4 million people. About half the counties in the country participated.

Wartime all but eliminated the problem of surplus food disposal, as well as unemployment and its attendant poverty, and the program was terminated. Almost immediately, however, agitation began in the Senate to reestablish food stamps, led unsuccessfully by Senators George Aiken (D-Vt.) and Robert La Follette Jr. (R-Wis.). In the 1950s, Representative Leonor Sullivan (D-Mo.) began a long crusade in the House on behalf of food stamps. Her efforts bore fruit in a 1959 amendment to a farm bill that authorized but did not mandate the secretary of agriculture to establish a food stamp program. USDA chose to ignore this authority until John F. Kennedy became president.

As a senator, Kennedy had himself introduced one of the many food stamp bills brought before Congress in the 1950s, and a commitment to food stamps was included in the platform of the Democratic party in the 1960 campaign. Given Kennedy's clear predilection for foreign policy, however, it is perhaps surprising that one of his very first actions was to issue an executive order to expand the distribution of food to needy families. Kennedy instructed the secretary of agriculture "to take immediate steps to expand and improve the program of food distribution throughout the United States," not only to help people in "areas of chronic unemployment" but also to strengthen farm prices.[4] A week later, basing his authority on the 1959 Sullivan amendment, the president informed Congress that he had ordered the secretary of agriculture to set up a pilot food stamp program in West Virginia, Pennsylvania, eastern Kentucky, northern Minnesota, southern Illinois, and Detroit.[5]

In 1963 the administration moved to continue the program but to shift the funding from the limited section 32 tariff revenues to regular appropriations, a change that would make it possible eventually to expand the program substantially. Sullivan introduced the bill.[6] Various versions of the legislation were debated over the course of the following year, as liberal urban Democrats sought to break up an opposing combine of Republicans and conservative rural Democrats. After Kennedy's assassination, Lyndon Johnson embraced the expansion of food stamps as a part of his War on Poverty, and congressional Democrats finally managed to fashion a winning intraparty coalition of urban northerners and rural southerners by offering to trade support for a wheat and cotton bill for passage of a food stamp bill. Congress finally established a permanent program in the summer of 1964, and the president signed the bill into law on August 31.

The legislation permitted states to choose whether to participate in the program. Originally, the law also allowed those states that chose to take part to set their own eligibility standards and to specify the counties in which the program would be available. This nod to states' rights led to striking inequities. Some states set food stamp eligibility to coincide with welfare eligibility, but other states established a much higher income floor. Everywhere, large numbers of people below the poverty line were not eligible to participate. A study by the Consumers Union calculates that among those states taking part in the program in 1970, the maximum monthly income allowable to qualify for food stamps ranged from 38 percent of the federal poverty line (in South Carolina) to 86 percent (in New Jersey).[7] At least seven states refused altogether to take part, but even where states accepted the program, availability at the county level varied sharply. In 1969 slightly fewer than half the counties in the United States were participating, making food stamps accessible to only 59 percent of the population.[8]

Congress addressed these issues first in the 1970 amendments to the original act that set uniform national income and resource eligibility standards and then in further amendments in 1973 that mandated that if a state took part in the program, then all counties had to offer food stamps. By 1975 food stamps were available in every state and county.

The initial program required recipients to make a cash purchase of food stamps at face value, the amount of which was determined by the family's income and size. Households were required to spend some cash income for the stamps. Even the very poorest had to lay out a token cash

payment. Then they received an allotment of free stamps supposedly sufficient to make possible the purchase of a low-cost diet developed by
USDA. Many recipients could not amass the necessary cash payment each
month, however, and some lived entirely outside a cash economy, particularly in the rural South. Efforts to eliminate the cash purchase requirement
began almost immediately after the 1964 act was passed, but it was not
until 1977 that it was abolished. Today households are expected to spend
30 percent of their net cash income, if they have any, directly for food.
Stamps then make up the gap between any cash expenditure and the price
of the current low-cost USDA diet known as the Thrifty Food Plan.
Eligibility extends to citizens with a gross monthly household income that
does not exceed 130 percent of the federal poverty line.[9]

Although the 1977 law led to significant increases in program participation, other provisions of the same law suggest the depth of legislative
ambivalence that has encumbered the food stamp program from its incep-
tion.[10] The same law that liberalized food stamps by making them available
to people who could not raise the cash purchase price also eliminated
automatic eligibility for households receiving AFDC or Supplemental
Security Income (SSI), a provision rescinded eight years later in the Food
Security Act of 1985. The 1977 restriction, however, removed more than
half a million people from the food stamp rolls.[11] In addition, new provisions lowered the effective net income ceiling for eligibility.

Changes passed by Congress early in the Reagan administration tem-
porarily stemmed the growth of the program by reducing benefits, establishing a gross income ceiling of 130 percent of the poverty line, and ending the eligibility of strikers and most college students. Between those
reforms and the welfare changes of 1996, however, Congress steadily liberalized eligibility. The 1985 Food Security Act not only made welfare recipients automatically eligible but increased the limits on liquid assets that a
household could hold. Assistance to the homeless was improved in 1987 by
the Stewart B. McKinney Homeless Assistance Act, and benefits were
increased across the board by the Hunger Prevention Act of 1988. Benefits
were increased again by the Mickey Leland Childhood Hunger Relief Act
in 1993, which also allowed higher deductions for high shelter costs. The
combination of broader eligibility and the recession during the Bush presidency drove food stamp numbers to record levels in the early 1990s. Not
only was a greater proportion of the American population enrolled in the
program than ever before (10.5 percent in 1994), but a higher proportion

Table 4-1. *Characteristics of Food Stamp Participants, 1992*

Characteristic	Percent
Below the federal poverty level	76.9
With AFDC income	48.9
With SSI income	27.6
In female-headed households	53.0
White	60.8
Black	34.2
Hispanic (of any race)	20.3
Under 18 years of age	52.1

Sources: AFDC and SSI data are 1995 data from *1996 Green Book*, Committee Print, House Committee on Ways and Means, 104 Cong. 2 sess. (Government Printing Office, 1996), p. 855. All other data are 1992 data from Bureau of the Census, *Statistical Abstract of the United States, 1997*, p. 376.

of the poor were taking advantage (72.1 percent in 1994, up from roughly 60 percent in the 1980s).[12]

By the 1990s the food stamp program was clearly targeted at the most needy among the low-income population. About 70 percent of food stamp recipients derived their income from public assistance programs, mainly AFDC and SSI. Female-headed households with children made up a slight majority of all recipients; the elderly comprised slightly less than one-fifth of those taking part in the program.[13] Ninety percent of food stamp recipients had gross incomes at or below the federal poverty line. As of 1992, 61 percent of those on the food stamp rolls were white (see table 4-1).[14]

Whose Interests Should the Food Stamp Program Serve?

To be able to show that food stamp assistance promotes the interests of those other than the hungry accords with a fundamental principle of political coalition-building and helps to account for the success of the program in Congress over the years.[15] The diversity of parties with a stake in food stamps has afforded the program a modest protective cover. Frequently, however, the program is revealed for what it is—a form of welfare assistance whose ultimate purpose is primarily humanitarian. In such instances, the food stamp program becomes subject to the doubts, opposition, and ambivalence that bear more broadly on the provision of social welfare.

Furthermore, problems have arisen (particularly in the early years of the program) when the interests of nonpoor beneficiaries—farmers and retail grocers, for example—clashed with those of the hungry.

From their initial appearance in the late Depression years through the establishment of the program in 1964, food stamps were seen as a means not simply of feeding the hungry but of creating a market for surplus farm products. Indeed, Barbara Claffey and Thomas Stuckey have argued that market support was the principal purpose of the program: "Alleviating hunger never commanded as high a priority as increasing farm income."[16] Others have concurred with this judgment. Noting that food assistance programs have been administered by USDA since 1935, William Boehm, Paul Nelson, and Kathryn Longen assert that "such programs were operated largely as mechanisms for surplus removal, designed primarily to help support farm income."[17] Janet Poppendieck seems to suggest that, at least at the beginning, dealing with surpluses and helping the hungry were coequal objectives of the Depression-era food assistance efforts.[18] As she observes elsewhere, however, the transfer of the originally independent Federal Surplus Relief Corporation to USDA in 1935 "marked the beginning of the process by which food assistance was increasingly divorced from federal relief and integrated with the Agriculture Department's price support programs for commercial agriculture."[19] Agricultural interests soon superseded the needs of the poor and the unemployed.[20] When the issue of reestablishing a food stamp program arose during the Eisenhower administration, USDA successfully resisted the idea on the grounds that commodity distribution was a more effective way of disposing of seasonal or localized surpluses than food stamps.

The purported benefits to agriculture were a central theme in the congressional debate over the establishment of a permanent food stamp program in 1964. Although a few of its proponents argued that the intent of food stamps was emphatically not to reduce surpluses but to help the poor eat well, most, including Leonor Sullivan herself, offered justifications that invoked the agricultural stake.[21] "The people who are on the [pilot] food stamp program are now buying meat which they could not afford to buy before," Sullivan noted. "By buying more meat, they are helping to use up more feed grains fed to cattle. That means less surplus grain."[22] Others pressed the idea that enhancing the food-buying power of the poor would unleash an "untapped major market," a large portion of whose expenditures would go to farmers.[23]

Subsequent studies backed up these claims. According to calculations done by USDA's Economic Research Service in 1975, for example, elimination of the food stamp program would reduce total expenditures on food in the United States by 1.5 to 2 percent. Families receiving food stamps were especially prone to spend more on meat, generating an annual net additional demand of about $1 billion. Retail stores and farmers were prime beneficiaries of increased household food consumption, with the latter getting about 42 cents of each additional retail food dollar spent through the food stamp program.[24]

Nevertheless, Republican and southern Democratic opponents of the program had fought food stamps in part for its failure to deplete surplus food stocks.[25] "These people with stamps can go into stores and buy caviar," Representative Charles Hoeven (R-Iowa) complained on the floor of the House. "They can buy a lot of things that are not in surplus. . . . We are not going to solve our surplus problem with this kind of legislation."[26] The Food Stamp Act, "purely a welfare bill" in the eyes of many, appeared simply to replace an effective agriculture support program—government purchase and distribution of surplus foods—with a taxpayer subsidy of "food that may not all be necessary to the maintenance of human life."[27] As a form of welfare, food stamps in this view should at least have been housed in the Department of Health, Education, and Welfare, not in Agriculture.

Three decades after the passage of the Food Stamp Act, the argument that food assistance to the hungry offered a vehicle to absorb surplus food and maintain farm prices had little currency. Indeed, such justifications had rarely been invoked in the intervening years; congressional debate over program extension and reform had instead focused narrowly on other issues. But in the early 1990s a series of congressional hearings on hunger revealed a continuing need to justify food stamps and other programs of hunger assistance on broader grounds, namely, in this instance, the argument that hungry people made it more difficult for the nation to compete in the global economy and to protect itself in the international order.

Dr. Aaron Shirley, a Mississippi civil rights activist from the early days of the movement, set the tone in hearings before the House Select Committee on Hunger: "It is a good investment to see to it that especially our children have adequate nutrition so that they can grow up to be productive citizens, they can be good soldiers, they can push the right button on the missile thing."[28] Representative Robin Tallon (D-S.C.) echoed this view several days later in opening another set of hearings: "Childhood hunger is not simply a matter of feeding hungry mouths, it is a case for National security and competitiveness."[29] And Representative Mike Espy (D-Miss.) worried that a generation of malnourished Americans would create a work force unable to compete with other nations, a view supported by the chairman of the Committee on Nutrition of the American Academy of Pediatrics.[30]

Some witnesses were clearly taken aback at this line of argument: "I think you need to look at what are the goals of your food programs," a social service administrator told the House Select Committee on Hunger. "Are you responding to some sort of a moral responsibility that you feel that society and government have to meet basic needs of the population? Or, are you responding to the fact that hungry school children cannot concentrate on their studies and miss basic living skills later in life that will lead them into dependency?"[31] For Representative Leon Panetta (D-Calif.), as for most of his colleagues, the answer, dictated by political realities, was easy: "Unfortunately, it is not enough to say we're feeding kids, we're feeding people, we're helping people. . . . We have to be much more definitive about what kind of return there is to the American society for making that kind of investment."[32]

Justifying food stamps and other food assistance on grounds other than humanitarian aid to the hungry creates certain problems. Although tying food stamps to agricultural interests had historically served to broaden the number of political stakeholders in the program, several inefficiencies and potentially disadvantageous tradeoffs arise from the fact that food stamps remain under the jurisdiction of the congressional agriculture committees. Food stamps must always compete in committee with agriculture price supports and other farm programs not at all connected to welfare. Although many representatives from farm states eventually came to be counted among the ardent supporters of food stamps, Sullivan nevertheless was led once to complain, "The House Agriculture Committee . . . treats [food stamps] like dirt . . . , an abomination that must be tolerated as the price for getting urban cooperation in the House on farm subsidy legislation."[33]

Another problem is that divided legislative jurisdiction over welfare programs makes coordination of the whole package of income assistance initiatives difficult.[34] Asked to give her advice on how to reform food stamps, an out-going USDA official told Congress that the one thing that most needed change in her view was the fragmented welfare service system: clients were sent to different offices to apply for food stamps, AFDC, WIC, medicaid, and other income maintenance programs. "It's a large challenge," she observed, "because the rules are written by the various authorizing committees."[35]

Justifying food stamps on investment and competitiveness grounds is also problematic. For one thing, it assumes that domestic food aid will in fact enhance global economic competitiveness, a proposition exceedingly difficult to evaluate. In addition, the investment argument also creates the expectation of some sort of quid pro quo on the part of recipients to the effect that if society "invests" in their well-being, they owe society some sort of return in the form of higher productivity, self-reliance, or achievement. If food stamps are predicated on such an exchange, many recipients are bound to fail, an outcome that can only diminish support for the program.

Fraud and Abuse

Ever since the depression-era food stamp program began, people have thought that cheating is widespread.[36] Public concerns are not without foundation. Some recipients have always been willing to sell their stamps at a discount for cash, and unscrupulous retailers have always been willing to buy them, later cashing in the stamps at full value. Recipients of stamps have also found it relatively easy to misrepresent their income or assets and thus claim assistance for which they are not eligible. Although perceptions of the extent of fraud tend to be significantly exaggerated, even the most ardent supporters of the program are willing to grant that it is a costly problem. The cost is not simply monetary, however; fraud of any magnitude also renders the program politically vulnerable, for it is easy to generate public and official outrage at reports of cheaters profiting at the expense of honest, working, taxpaying people.[37] Charges of fraud and abuse have therefore often provided a politically inexpensive way for hostile members of Congress to mobilize opposition to the program, enabling them to avoid the far riskier and apparently mean-spirited strategy of opposing food aid to hungry people altogether.

Investigations of fraud and abuse are not only easy ways to arouse public and congressional anger, but they also divert attention from the more serious problems that food stamps encounter, such as low participation rates and administrative complexity, the solution to which might result in larger food stamp rolls.[38] The first hearings conducted by the full House Agriculture Committee after party control shifted to the Republicans in

Table 4-2. *Average Monthly Food Stamp Participation Rates, 1964–95*
Millions

Year	Number	Year	Number
1964	0.33	1980	19.22
1965	0.42	1981	20.63
1966	0.86	1982	19.90
1967	1.44	1983	21.62
1968	2.20	1984	20.85
1969	2.87	1985	19.90
		1986	19.43
1970	4.34	1987	19.11
1971	9.37	1988	18.64
1972	11.11	1989	18.76
1973	12.17		
1974	12.86	1990	19.93
1975	16.26	1991	22.57
1976	17.02	1992	25.37
1977	15.60	1993	27.00
1978	14.50	1994	27.50
1979	15.89	1995	26.60

Source: *1996 Green Book*, Committee Print, p. 874.

1994 was devoted, for example, not to the larger issue of the role of food stamps in the impending reform of the welfare system but to food stamp fraud, a problem that had to be addressed first, according to the committee chair.[39]

In the 1970s opponents attacked the program by arguing that generous eligibility standards permitted huge numbers of well-off people to obtain food stamps. The assault took shape in the context of sharply rising participation rates, stimulated by high unemployment and increasing food costs after the Arab oil embargo of 1973 (see table 4-2).[40] Even as Congress debated reforms such as the establishment of national eligibility standards and reduction of the cash purchase price for the very poor, hostile members of Congress sought to focus the debate instead on college students and strikers on the food stamp rolls. Although good data were never collected that indicated the national extent of participation by either group, amendments were introduced repeatedly from 1969 to 1977 seeking to bar what various legislators claimed were "children of wealthy parents," "students with brand new automobiles," and "people involved in voluntary work stoppages."[41] Eventually, students and strikers were blocked from participation unless they meet other eligibility requirements.

The belief that college students routinely used food stamps was part of a broader conviction that "affluent families" were taking advantage of the program.[42] Representative Robert Daniel (D-Va.) claimed that "the owners of jewelry, furs, and luxury appliances" could get food stamps.[43] Senator Charles Grassley (R-Iowa) claimed that "millions of taxpayers' dollars are going down the drain because of people of means getting on the program."[44]

In fact, most users of food stamps have always been found among the ranks of the poor. Even as the debate over students, strikers, and the affluent was going on, USDA data showed that the vast bulk of families receiving food stamps in 1975 fell below the federal poverty line of $5,500 for a nonfarm family of four. Only 13 percent of families on food stamps earned more than $6,000 per year; most of these were in families with five or more people where the poverty threshold was $6,499. The maximum net income for food stamp eligibility (after allowable deductions) for families of five was $7,560.[45]

As Congress sought to respond to concerns about abuse by the well-to-do by restricting eligibility, opponents of food stamps were portraying the program as a "haven for . . . ripoff artists."[46] Charges that outright fraud was rapidly increasing appeared in the press.[47] As early as 1973, however, USDA officials had assured Congress that the incidence of fraud was low: USDA investigations had found only $28,000 lost through the illegal sale of food stamps at a discount (trafficking). The proportion of fraudulently participating households, it was said, was only .0024 percent of all participants.[48] In 1974 USDA reported the incidence of household fraud at just .08 percent. These figures became the accepted estimates of fraud until a General Accounting Office investigation found in fact that no accurate nationwide data on recipient fraud or trafficking were available.[49]

Although USDA and other federal officials have continued to maintain that the incidence of fraud is relatively small, comprehensive data remain elusive. By the middle of the 1990s, however, GAO was able to provide some realistic assessments of the dimensions of various types of food stamp fraud. GAO distinguishes among four types of fraud: counterfeiting, mail theft, trafficking, and eligibility fraud. Neither of the first two, they say, is a significant problem. They estimate that between 1986 and 1992 counterfeit food stamps amounted to only about $1.2 million. The rational counterfeiter is unwilling to expend the effort to manufacture coupons that fetch only 50 or 60 percent of their modest face value. Nor

Table 4-3. *Estimates of Fraud and Abuse in the Food Stamp Program*

Year	Percent
Participating retail food stores disqualified from the program for trafficking[a]	
1973	0.022
1992	1.45
Fraudulently participating households (estimated)[b]	
1973	0.024
1974	0.08
1992	0.76

a. *Food Stamp Trafficking and the Food Stamp Electronic Benefit Program*, Joint Hearing, 102 Cong. 2 sess. (GPO, March 15, 1992), p. 8. In 1973, 400 out of 180,000 stores were disqualified, while in 1992, 3,200 out of 220,000 were disqualified.

b. Estimates for 1973 and 1974 come from *The Food Stamp Controversy of 1975*, Committee Print, Senate Select Committee on Nutrition and Human Needs, 94 Cong. 1 sess. (GPO, October 1975), p. 45; the 1992 figure is calculated on the basis of the General Accounting Office estimate of about 195,000 cases of recipient fraud in 1992 out of a total of more than 25 million participants. See GAO, *Food Assistance: Reducing Fraud and Abuse in the Food Stamp Program with Electronic Benefit Transfer Technologies* (GPO, February 2, 1994), p. 3.

is mail theft especially costly. Of the slightly more than $6 billion in stamps distributed by mail in 1992, less than .5 percent ($22.5 million) was lost. How much of this loss was due to theft and how much to genuine loss is not known.[50]

The cost of trafficking is also unknown. Although USDA's Office of the Inspector General offers data on the number of retail stores that have been disqualified from participating in the food stamp program for trafficking (table 4-3), much of this type of fraud involves such small sums of money that it is never detected. The Office of the Inspector General has refused to guess at the cost.[51]

Eligibility fraud, the illegal acquisition of food stamps by recipients through deception or misrepresentation, is the sort of fraud that particularly angers the public and its political representatives. GAO has long been able to calculate overpayments to recipients. Overpayments as a percentage of food stamp expenditures declined between 1977 and 1993 (see table 4-4). Only in recent years has the agency been able to break down this dollar loss into caseworker error, inadvertent recipient error, and overt recipient fraud. In the period 1988–93 overpayments amounted to $7.4 billion, of which $1.8 billion was due to recipient fraud, that is, slightly less than one-quarter

Table 4-4. *Total Overpayments as a Percentage of All Food Stamp Expenditures, Selected Years, 1977–93*[a]

Year	Percent
1977	12.0
1980	10.4
1983	8.2
1985	8.3
1990	7.3
1993	7.8

Sources: The 1977 figure comes from GAO, *The Food Stamp Program—Overissued Benefits Not Recovered and Fraud Not Punished*, Report to Congress (GPO, July 18, 1977); 1980 and 1983 figures come from GAO, *Food Assistance: Reducing Fraud and Abuse*; 1985 and 1990 figures are from Department of Agriculture, Food and Nutrition Service, *Evaluating the Hunger Prevention Act Quality Control Reforms*, a report to Congress prepared by Abt Associates (GPO, September 1991), p. 14; and the figure for 1993 is calculated on the basis of data contained in *Enforcement of the Food Stamp Program*, Hearings before the House Committee on Agriculture, 104 Cong. 1 sess. (GPO, February 1, 1995), p. 6.

a. Figures include caseworker error, inadvertent recipient error, and recipient fraud.

of all overpayments. In 1993 such recipient fraud totaled 1 to 2 percent of all food stamp expenditures.[52]

Some proponents of the food stamp program have been defensive about food stamp fraud, arguing that compared with the total cost of the program the amount of fraud is relatively modest.[53] Others have sought to hold the accusers accountable for their charges. When Secretary William Simon charged that the food stamp program was a haven for rip-off artists, Senator George McGovern (D-S.D.) invited him to back up his statements in testimony before the Senate Select Committee on Nutrition and Human Needs or to retract his attack.[54] Still other proponents have understood the power of fraud and abuse charges to distract the nation and the Congress from the real purpose of the program, namely, to feed hungry people.[55] When fraud hearings and charges receive nothing more than routine press coverage, the relief of food stamp proponents is palpable.[56]

Participation in the Food Stamp Program

From the very beginning of the modern food stamp program, large numbers of eligible people have not taken part. Although nonparticipation is no longer the mystery it once was, it remains a source of continuing concern for public officials and anti-hunger advocates. Ironically, it was thought that the food stamp program would eliminate the impediments to participation that plagued the system of direct surplus commodity distribution, the main form of food aid in the 1950s. The inconvenience of once-a-month distribution at a central warehouse and the monotony of the limited variety of foods, such as cornmeal, dried beans, and cheese, often in unusably large quantities difficult to transport home and to store, discouraged many from participating.[57] But when counties began to switch from commodity distribution to food stamps in the initial pilot program, the number of eligible people seeking food aid actually fell off.[58]

Public officials finally came to the conclusion that the need to lay out cash to purchase a food stamp allotment, a requirement that contrasted unfavorably with the free commodity distribution program, prevented some from taking part. But the purchase requirement has long since been eliminated and still the food stamp program fails to enroll between a third and a quarter of all eligible recipients.

Calculating participation rates is not a simple matter. The most accurate method of determining the number of participants is to use administrative data. To get a participation *rate*, however, the number of eligibles must be inferred from survey data. Many studies, committed to drawing both the numerator and the denominator from the same source, use survey data to estimate participants as well, but this substantially underestimates real food stamp participation.[59] The best survey source for extrapolating the number of eligibles is the Survey of Income and Program Participation (SIPP), which collects more of the information necessary to determine eligibility than, say, the Current Population Survey (CPS) or the Panel Survey on Income Dynamics (PSID). But SIPP first went into the field in 1983, forcing those interested in tracking long-term participation trends to use either of these two less satisfactory surveys for the denominator.

One analysis using data from program administrative files on participation and SIPP to get at eligibility shows that food stamp participation among individuals increased between 1985 and 1992 from 64.3 percent of eligibles to 73.8 percent.[60] The sharp rise in participation at the beginning of the 1990s contrasts with a relatively steady rate in the 60 percent range during the previous decade. The number of nonparticipant eligibles was estimated in 1992 at 8.6 million.[61]

Participation is highest among children under five years of age (95 percent of eligibles are enrolled) and lowest among the elderly (33 percent).

The rate of participation in the program is higher as household income decreases. Because registering for food stamps may involve multiple trips to a social services office and submission to a detailed and intrusive set of questions, people seem to take into account some sort of benefit-cost ratio: they are much more likely to undertake registering for the program when their food stamp benefits are relatively high.[62] Nearly all eligible black households receive food stamps (92 percent), but only 61 percent of eligible Hispanic and 59 percent of eligible white households do.[63] Alberto Martini has found, however, that black and white female-headed households participate at similar rates.[64] The best predictor of food stamp receipt is enrollment in AFDC or SSI.[65]

Single-adult households with children tend to stay on food stamps longer than other recipients, and when they go off the program they also have the highest recidivism rate.[66] Nancy Burstein's analysis of SIPP data found that most people are enrolled in the program for less than a year at a time: about two-thirds of recipients left within twelve months. But she also found that one-third of these later returned to the program. The mean spell on stamps was twenty months. Another study, also based on SIPP data, estimated that of the 18.8 million people on food stamps in 1987, 62 percent were still enrolled twenty-eight months later.[67]

The roots of most nonparticipation appear to lie in a failure of public policy. Richard Coe found, for example, that the major reason for failure to register for food stamps among the elderly and the working poor was simply lack of information about eligibility.[68] "This implies," Coe writes, "that efforts are needed to inform these groups that the Food Stamp Program is a universal means-tested income support program and is open to those who have jobs and to households that contain no dependent children."[69]

The Physician Task Force on Hunger in America was also convinced that the numerous, ever-changing, and overly complex administrative rules that govern eligibility were designed by the federal government to discourage and intimidate potential recipients. Although "one cannot be certain about conscious motivation," the task force report notes, "using bureaucracy to prevent entitlements . . . is seen by state food stamp administrators as being deliberate on the part of the federal government."[70] A survey done by GAO in the mid-1980s lends credence to this view. GAO analysts found that about one-third of households eligible for food stamps but not enrolled in the program explained their nonparticipation by citing either burdensome administrative requirements (such as being required to come into the food stamp office more than once, having to supply complete documentation of income, assets, and living costs) or problems of access to the office itself (such as limited hours, distance from home).[71]

Reluctance to face the presumed social disapproval directed at recipients of government assistance also accounts for some nonparticipation. Food stamps, virtual cash equivalents redeemed at the checkout counter in retail food stores, were originally thought of as a way to spare recipients the embarrassment of standing in a public line to receive commodity donations. But in fact the food stamp transaction is also open to public view, and many recipients report embarrassment at having to use such assistance. A GAO survey in the mid-1980s found that 14 percent of the sample of eligibles cited embarrassment as the main reason for their nonparticipation.[72] A survey done among a sample of eligible elderly people in New York, Oregon, and South Carolina in 1981 found an identical proportion saying they were too embarrassed or too proud to apply for food stamps.[73]

The stigma associated with food stamp use is an artifact of ambivalent public attitudes toward social welfare, which are not easily influenced by policy.[74] But the information deficit that accounts for the bulk of nonparticipation can be remedied by effective outreach programs. The history of outreach efforts, however, has been spotty.

In the early years of the modern food stamp program, Congress required state agencies to encourage participation and aggressively inform eligible nonparticipants of their entitlement.[75] Washington provided matching funds to support these activities and assigned USDA responsibility for making sure that state welfare agencies initiated outreach programs. Failure to do so would result in the loss of food stamp dollars. States were supposed to file outreach plans with USDA by January 1, 1972, but most of them, reluctant to put up the required 40 percent of the cost, failed to do so.[76]

Food stamp advocates brought a class action suit in federal court to force the states to comply with the law. In *Bennett* v. *Butz* the court instructed USDA to require the states to appoint full-time outreach coordinators and to produce monthly reports on progress in enrolling eligible nonparticipants.[77] But mandatory outreach efforts came to an abrupt end in the Reagan era: the Omnibus Budget Reconciliation Act of 1981 ended all outreach provisions in food stamp legislation and forbade the use of federal funds for such activities, including informing low-income households of their eligibility, publicizing application requirements and procedures, and advertising the benefits of food stamps.

With the passage of the 1987 Stewart B. McKinney Homeless Assistance Act, however, Congress began to back off from this uncompromising position by providing federal matching funds to state agencies, which could, at their option, implement outreach programs for the homeless. Even broader outreach programs, supported by federal and state matching funds, were authorized subsequently:

— The 1988 Hunger Prevention Act provided federal money to states that wished to inform low-income households of their eligibility for food stamps.

— The 1990 farm bill authorized USDA to conduct demonstration outreach projects.

— In 1991 the Food and Nutrition Service (called the Food and Consumer Service from 1993 to early 1998), the USDA agency that administers food stamps, announced a small-grants competition for both public and nonprofit service providers, often in partnership, to demonstrate innovative outreach techniques.

— In 1994 Congress committed $500,000 to the Social Security Administration to add food stamp information for the elderly to a demonstration SSI outreach program.

Despite these developments, outreach, once a mandatory feature of the food stamp program, remains optional, and programs are almost entirely of the demonstration type. Even though lack of information and confusing application procedures remain formidable barriers to participation, particularly among the elderly, non-English speakers, the working poor, the rural poor, and the disabled, outreach demonstration projects are found in only about half the states.[78] Some of these states have not renewed their own funding contribution after the completion of the demonstration projects.

Adequacy Issues

Few would argue that food stamps provide a generous subsidy; many in fact contend that the allotment the program offers is inadequate. Food stamp recipients often complain that the stamps run out by the third week of the month, and policy analysts point out that many features of program administration undercut the intended purchasing power of the stamps.

Neither the pilot program of 1961 nor the statutory program of 1964 was designed to provide enough stamps to people at the bottom end of the income distribution to guarantee that they could buy a complete diet, according to Jeffrey Berry. The stamps provided more food but not necessarily enough to ensure consumption even of the USDA Economy Food Plan, what was then the lowest cost diet.[79] The Economy Food Plan itself set an extremely low standard of adequacy: nutritionists regarded it as "essentially for emergency use."[80]

A lawsuit in 1975 claiming that USDA was failing to fulfill the requirements of the 1964 act to provide "an opportunity more nearly to obtain a nutritionally adequate diet" forced the department to replace the Economy Food Plan, low in cost but high in sugar and fats, with a Thrifty Food Plan.[81] The cost of this plan became the basis for food stamp allotments after 1977.

Since that date, maximum food stamp benefits have been set at between 99 percent and 103 percent of the cost of the Thrifty Food Plan. That is to say, 30 percent of the food stamp household's cash income plus the stamp allotment should allow virtual purchase of this basic diet. The plan meets minimum recommended daily allowances for key nutrients. The cost of the Thrifty Food Plan and food stamp benefits are adjusted for inflation in food prices.

Various studies indicate that food stamp use has positive nutritional impacts, which at first glance suggests that the program offers an adequate subsidy. An analysis by researchers at the Tufts Center on Hunger, Poverty and Nutrition Policy found that low-income children in food stamp families have better nutrition than low-income children in families that do not use food stamps, although the study does not control for any income variations, access to other food assistance programs, place of residence, family composition, or any other demographic variable.[82] Barbara Devaney and Robert Moffitt control for cash income, the size of the food stamp benefit, place of residence, age, and other factors and find that "household availability of all nutrients" is positively related to food stamp use.[83] James Ohls and Harold Beebout conclude that food stamps do "reasonably well" to make sure that poor people can buy enough food to provide a basically healthy diet.[84]

These assessments, however, mask a number of problems that diminish the ability of all stamp recipients to buy the full Thrifty Food Plan. For example, the stamp allotment is geared only to the size of the household. A unit with two teenage boys receives the same amount of subsidy as a unit with two infants, controlling for cash income, even though consumption requirements of the former are much greater.

Several investigations have shown that since food stamp allotments do not take geographical price differences into account, many recipients find the food stamp subsidy insufficient to purchase the basic Thrifty Food Plan market basket. In rural areas, for example, consumers must often rely on more expensive "mom and pop" food stores or monopoly supermarkets. The rural poor, according to one study, would need on average a 17 percent increase in their food stamp allotment to buy the full Thrifty Food Plan.[85] Prices are also higher in large cities and in high-poverty neighborhoods. Buyers from the Food Research and Action Center found that on a monthly basis food stamps fell between $25 and $42 short of the full purchase price of the food plan in eight of the ten supermarkets they visited.[86] Lack of competition among retail food stores, the higher cost of doing business in poor areas, and the scale of retail operations all help to account for the higher prices in stores that serve the rural and inner city poor. But part of the shortfall is an artifact of the inflation adjustment procedures. Although the cost of the Thrifty Food Plan is adjusted monthly, food stamp benefits are adjusted only about once a year, producing a lag that may run as high as fifteen months behind the real cost of food purchases.[87]

Congress has also been willing, in the interests of budget reduction, to modify the Thrifty Food Plan baseline standard. When USDA adopted the food plan in 1977, maximum food stamp benefits were set at 100 percent of the cost of that diet. In 1982, however, Congress reduced the maximum to 99 percent of the food plan's cost, although it was increased to 100 percent again in 1984. The Hunger Prevention Act of 1988 actually gradually raised the baseline allotment to 103 percent of the Thrifty Food Plan, but Congress rolled this back to 100 percent in the welfare changes embodied in the Personal Responsibility and Work Opportunity Reconciliation Act of 1996. These minor, often symbolic, seemingly mean-spirited changes are not inconsequential for low-income food buyers, where stamps and dollars must be used at maximum levels of efficiency to provide for an adequate diet. Few households operate at these levels, however. The cost of the Thrifty Food Plan is calibrated taking into account assumptions about levels of food wastage in the average household and time available to prepare meals from basic ingredients that do not accord with actual living patterns. For example, in calculating the cost of the Thrifty Food Plan, USDA assumes that 5 percent of the food that comes into a household is discarded through spoilage or plate waste, but most studies indicate that a much higher percentage is typically lost.

Even if demographic, geographical, and administrative adjustments were made to enable recipients to buy the full Thrifty Food Plan, food stamps remain vulnerable to congressional budget-cutting. In the Personal Responsibility and Work Opportunity Reconciliation Act of 1996, or welfare reform, Congress enacted huge cuts. Indeed, half the spending reductions in these reforms come from the food stamps, effected in large part by freezing the standard deduction from cash income, formerly indexed to inflation, at 1996 levels.[88] The effect is to reduce the average food stamp benefit per person per meal from 80 cents to 66 cents.

Conclusions

In theory a means-tested national entitlement program that provides a sufficient subsidy to eligible households to buy a basic nutritious diet should be the instrument to end all food insecurity in the United States. In practice, however, the program has fallen well short of this goal. The food stamp program has a history of grudging assistance that many believe is inadequate. Congressional renewal and reform as well as program administration seem often to have been shaped as much by the determination to bar cheaters as to conquer food deprivation. Given the size of the program, it has often been an attractive target for congressional budget cutting, a goal accomplished by restricting eligibility, eliminating categories of recipients, or diminishing the baseline diet on which the subsidy is calculated.

The food stamp program has endured, of course, for more than three decades. Even with the changes wrought in 1996, it is still a more generous program than it once was. Nevertheless, food stamps sit at the pivot point between American society's compassion for hungry people and its disdain for public welfare. Torn between these opposing forces, the program, as it has been run, is an imperfect answer to the problem of food insecurity in the United States.

5 Filling in the Gaps: The Targeted Food Assistance Programs

The judgment rendered about the food stamp program applies as well to many of the targeted food assistance programs, both individually and as a group: good design, problematic implementation. Besides food stamps, USDA administers an array of smaller programs that assume correctly that certain clienteles have special needs that a means-tested food voucher entitlement may not serve or may not serve well.[1] But like food stamps, these programs are generally underfunded. Many of these programs have had to fight for their survival, despite consistently positive assessments of their effectiveness. The histories of some of them are marked by sharp fluctuations in appropriations, and a number of the programs have been perennial targets of executive branch and congressional skeptics, who doubt their need and question the motives of their clients. Implementation of a few of the programs was slow to occur, frustrating congressional proponents.

The targeted programs are designed to protect particularly vulnerable or needy groups whose feeding and nutrition might not be guaranteed under the blunter device of food stamps (children, for example, cannot control the expenditure of food stamps in their households) or who cannot, for one reason or another, participate in the retail food economy, even with stamps. These special categories of beneficiaries include reservation Indians (who may not have access to grocery stores in which to redeem

Table 5-1. *Federal Domestic Food Assistance Programs, 1996*

Program	Expenditures (billions of dollars)	Number of participants (millions)
Food stamps	22.8	24.7
National school lunch	6.1	25.6
School breakfast	1.2	6.3
Child and adult care food	1.4	2.0
Summer food service	0.28	2.3
Special milk	0.017	a
Special supplemental food program for women, infants, and children (WIC)	3.1	7.4
Commodity supplemental food	0.007	0.4
The emergency food assistance program (TEFAP) and soup kitchens (SK) and food banks	0.19[b]	c
Food distribution on Indian reservations	0.42	0.12
Nutrition program for the elderly	0.15	d

Sources: Department of Agriculture Web site, Preliminary Summary of Food Assistance Program Results for September 1996; Victor Oliveira, "Spending on Food Assistance Programs Leveled off in 1995," *Food Review*, vol. 18 (September–December 1995), pp. 3–43; USDA, Food and Consumer Service, "TEFAP and SK Funding History," February 20, 1997.

a. School milk is served only in schools that do not participate in the school lunch or breakfast programs, except for kindergartens. USDA reports the numbers of half pints of milk service (152 million), not the numbers of participants.

b. The 1997 appropriation for the merged TEFAP and soup kitchen and food bank programs.

c. TEFAP services individuals; the soup kitchen and food bank program serves institutions. TEFAP served about 7.8 million people in 1996.

d. USDA counts the number of meals served (251 million), not the number of individual participants. Figures are for 1995.

stamps), pregnant women, infants, children in school, children on summer vacation, and the elderly poor.[2] In addition, USDA provides commodities to food banks and soup kitchens (see table 5-1). The conjunction of grudging implementation, growing demand, uneven funding, and positive evaluation is best understood through the stories of the individual programs.

Supplemental Food Programs

Perhaps because of its distinctive medical rationale, the special supplemental food program for women, infants, and children (WIC) has lent itself more readily to evaluation than have some of the other federal food assistance programs, whose objectives are primarily to ensure regular and adequate consumption. Certainly, none of these other programs has been studied as much as WIC. The results of these investigations are almost universally positive, though researchers differ to some degree on the magnitude of beneficial effects. Congress is generally aware of these positive evaluations and cites them regularly in renewing authorization for the program. Nevertheless, WIC has not always enjoyed the support of the federal executive branch. The result has been that for most of its history, WIC appropriations have been inadequate to meet demand.

Any understanding of WIC must begin with the conflict over this program between Congress and several presidential administrations. Although most accounts trace the origins of the program to the 1969 White House Conference on Food, Nutrition, and Health, officials from USDA and the Department of Health, Education, and Welfare had begun meeting as early as 1967 to discuss a program to augment the nutrition of low-income pregnant women and infants.[3] In 1968 the Citizens' Board of Inquiry into Hunger and Malnutrition announced its support for such an effort, and later that year Secretary of Agriculture Orville Freeman established a small supplemental food program to distribute surplus cereals, juices, and milk over and above the normal food stamp allowance to this high-risk group.[4] President Nixon then endorsed the supplemental food program at a White House conference, where it was declared that hunger and malnutrition among poor pregnant and lactating women and infants constituted a national emergency and demanded immediate relief. In response Congress established WIC as a two-year pilot program in 1972 and then as a permanent program in 1974 in amendments to the Child Nutrition Act of 1966.

Participation in WIC is open to pregnant and lactating women and children up to the age of five who are certified by medical personnel to be nutritionally "at-risk" and whose income is less than 185 percent of the federal poverty line.[5] States, which receive federal funding for WIC but administer the program through public or private nonprofit health agencies or clinics, may set lower income ceilings. WIC is not an entitlement program; thus participation is limited by the amount of funding appropriated by Congress, as well as any supplementary funds provided by the states. From the beginning, there has never been enough money to serve everyone who is eligible. Indeed, for a long time less than half of all eligible people were able to participate in WIC in any given year.[6] Funding increased significantly in the 1990s, however. In 1996 participation was

projected at 7.2 million people per month, although the number of people
eligible and likely to apply was estimated at between 7.5 million and 8 million.[7] The program is not very costly on a per capita basis: most recipients
receive on average only about $30 worth of food per month.[8]

A key element of the original legislation was a mandate to administering agencies to maintain medical records of program participants sufficient
to permit an evaluation of the nutritional benefits of the program. "One of
the purposes of WIC," as Senator Hubert Humphrey (D-Minn.) observed
in hearings on the early trials of the program, "is to get us a little more scientific data on what food supplements or what nutritional supplements can
do in terms of the physical and mental health of people."[9]

Both Congress and USDA were interested from the beginning in measuring the health outcomes of supplementary food assistance for women
and their children even before passage of the WIC program. Shortly after
Secretary Freeman ordered implementation of the supplemental food program, USDA commissioned a Cornell University research team to examine its effectiveness. The results of this modest study of projects in Bibb
County, Georgia, and Chicago were disappointing: recipients of surplus
foods seemed to fare no better nutritionally than a control group that used
only food stamps. Although Congress gathered testimony by scientists and
doctors in favor of continuing and expanding supplemental nutrition,
USDA decided to phase out the program. As Clayton Yeutter, assistant
secretary of USDA, commented before Congress, "Even if we make supplemental foods available as we have for the past few years, there is really
no guarantee or assurance . . . that those foods will be consumed. . . . Total
nutrient consumption changes little and perhaps none at all."[10]

USDA's skepticism about the supplemental food program carried over
to WIC and placed the department at odds with Congress for more than a
decade. USDA first refused to write regulations for the two-year pilot WIC
program, delaying its implementation. Agriculture officials explained their
inaction by asserting that WIC's medical objectives took precedence over
its feeding goals and thus made the program more appropriately the
responsibility of the Department of Health, Education, and Welfare.[11]
Congress believed that the law was clear, however: WIC was USDA's program, and the initial delay in issuing regulations represented, "for all practical purposes, a veto of the first year."[12] When USDA finally issued regulations, permitting the program to begin, they were confusing. For
example, cottage cheese, on the original list of acceptable foods, was suddenly deemed unacceptable, but state health agencies had by this time

already printed recipes for distribution that called for cottage cheese.[13] More troubling to nutritionists and to Congress was USDA's grudging decision to set the nutrient level for food allocated to pregnant women at 1,440 grams per month, even though the widely accepted National Academy of Sciences standard was 2,000 grams.[14]

Matters did not improve. Regulations governing the medical research were late being issued, which held up the initiation of an outcome evaluation that Congress had expected. Furthermore, USDA had refused to spend all the money Congress had appropriated, which meant that many projects approved by USDA had not yet served a single client. "The problems that bring us here today have a familiar cast to them," Senator McGovern commented in opening hearings before the Senate select committee in 1976. "Once again, the USDA is refusing to simply obey the law."[15]

USDA's reluctance to embrace WIC could not be justified by the early reports about the program's operations. The first evaluation of WIC implementation, commissioned by USDA's Food and Nutrition Service, took place after the program had been going for two years. Researchers found high levels of client satisfaction and noted that WIC participation tended to increase use of medical services. Clients generally ignored the nutrition education that accompanied WIC food assistance, however. The study also showed that slightly less than half the WIC participants received food stamps and even smaller percentages of families with school children received federal school breakfast and lunch aid. For most people, then, WIC was not a supplementary program, as its architects had intended it to be, but the sole source of food assistance.[16]

In 1978, shortly after the appearance of the Urban Institute report, Congress directed USDA to conduct a national study of WIC's nutritional and health-related outcomes and to report within thirty months. The history of USDA's management of this evaluation is a strange one. Many food assistance champions in Congress were in fact convinced that the department deliberately sought to sabotage a program that the Reagan administration did not wholly support.[17] The story was played out over the entire decade of the 1980s.

In response to the 1978 congressional mandate, the Food and Nutrition Service contracted with a North Carolina research institute to conduct the evaluation. After two years in the field, however, the department asked a new principal investigator to take over, at which point the field study was entirely redesigned. When USDA finally released the five-volume evaluation in 1986, which cost twice the original budget, it published only fifty copies, making it, according to Representative Tony Hall, "one of the rarest books in Congress these days."[18] What made members of Congress particularly angry, however, was not simply the high cost and tardiness of the report but that USDA had edited out the short executive and chapter summaries written by the authors of the report (without consulting them) and substituted different summaries, which were incomplete, inaccurate, and misleading.[19] Congress ordered the General Accounting Office to investigate the alteration of the evaluation study.

GAO did not report until 1990, at which point it found that USDA had indeed misrepresented the findings of the evaluation and even deleted conclusions that were favorable to WIC.[20] In response to the GAO findings, USDA officials, though refusing to speculate about the motives that led to the substitution of misleading chapter summaries, apologized to Congress.[21] Despite the effort to obscure the conclusions of the evaluation, however, the body of the USDA national WIC evaluation report provided strong support for judging the program a success.

USDA's decision to release only the heavily edited version prompted the study's authors in 1988 to publish independently their original findings in a special issue of the *American Journal of Clinical Nutrition*.[22] The investigation reported significant health benefits for WIC participants. Women who participated in WIC had longer pregnancies, lower rates of fetal mortality, fewer premature births, and larger babies. Compared with the control group, participants sought earlier prenatal medical care and improved their intake of various nutrients. WIC participation was also associated with better dietary intake among preschool children. Finally, WIC functioned as a genuine supplement to ordinary patterns of food acquisition, increasing the consumption of dairy and other qualifying foods.[23]

The beneficial effects of WIC in reducing the incidence of low-birth-weight babies is now a firmly established finding in the clinical literature. Sheila Avruch and Alicia Puente Cackley review sixteen studies, in addition to the national WIC evaluation, which were conducted between 1981 and 1991. All but three show statistically significant differences in the rate of low-weight births between WIC and non-WIC samples.[24] Basing their calculations on the average reduction in low birth weight and the cost of first-year medical care for low-birth-weight babies, the authors estimate that the WIC program averted $1.19 billion in first year medical expenditures in 1992 alone. Such findings led GAO to recommend that Congress make all pregnant women with incomes under 185 percent of the poverty line eligible for WIC foods, whether or not they are deemed to be nutritionally at risk, and to fund the program fully to cover all eligibles.[25]

The weight of clinical evidence attesting to the positive impact of the WIC program has made it a favorite in Congress. One staunch but lonely critic of the program speaks of the "widespread conviction [in Congress] that WIC is simply above reproach."[26] Senator Byron Dorgan (D-N.D.) has called WIC "one of the finest programs that we've ever developed at the Federal level," a view shared by many colleagues in both houses over the years.[27] Yet WIC has never been funded sufficiently to serve all eligible women and children. Although some of the responsibility for this failure must be borne by Congress, it was Congress that repeatedly saved the program when all during the decade of the 1980s efforts to cut WIC shifted from USDA to the White House.

The first Reagan budget sought to cut the Carter administration's request for WIC by 27 percent. In the end Congress restored most but not all of the cuts.[28] In 1982 the president proposed eliminating WIC altogether. States would be allowed to use funds from the expanded maternal and child health care block grant to provide nutrition assistance, but the monies from WIC would not be folded into the block grant. Congress rejected this plan.[29]

For more than a decade and a half, favorable evaluations of WIC were not sufficient to overcome skepticism or opposition in the executive branch of the federal government. Early USDA doubts seemed to stem from the belief that WIC was ineffective and unnecessary, while presidential opposition later on was part of the effort to dismantle the infrastructure of the welfare system. Congress did appear to respond to the good news about WIC, however, and its consistent support helped to protect the program. But WIC's staunchest congressional supporters were never able to break the delicate tension between support and opposition. Such tension allowed the program to be maintained but prevented it from achieving full funding or entitlement status. In the 1990s, WIC survived a threat by congressional Republicans to fold it into a block grant to the states. With the presidency in the hands of the Democrats, executive branch opposition to the program finally disappeared.

The Child Nutrition Programs

Proponents of the WIC program managed to articulate its objectives in a relatively focused, unambiguous way, but the justifications and goals of the five child nutrition programs—school lunch, school breakfast, special milk, summer food service, and child care—present a more complex story. While WIC has clearly been aimed at supplementing the nutritional intake of low-income women and infants deemed by health professionals to be at "nutritional risk," the early child food assistance programs involving lunch and milk were justified not only on nutritional grounds but also for their contribution to promoting national defense and absorbing surplus commodities. WIC has provided supplementary nutrition solely to low-income recipients, but some observers have always questioned whether the child nutrition programs should be universal but available on an ability-to-pay basis or reserved exclusively for means-tested recipients. The multiplicity and, to some extent, confusion of objectives have created a somewhat different political context for the child nutrition programs than for WIC. One curious manifestation of the difference was that WIC, a program with clear welfare goals, survived the Reagan-era budget cuts, while most of the childhood nutrition programs, none of which restrict participation to poor children, were severely cut.

But the early 1980s marked a brief moment of congressional disaffection. Except for an effort by House Republicans to consolidate all the child nutrition programs in 1995, bipartisan congressional support for these individual programs has been strong ever since.

Program assessments do not explain fully the budget history of lunch and breakfast programs, but they are crucial for understanding the treatment of the summer food service early in the Reagan administration. A series of investigations that focused not on its nutritional impacts but on administrative improprieties and mismanagement took place just prior to the Reagan presidency. These reports rendered summer food service vulnerable both in the Senate and the White House and thus suggest that the political dynamics that account for severe cuts in this program in the early 1980s were slightly different from those that affected the fate of the other child nutrition efforts.

School Food Programs

Public provision of lunch to children in school precedes all other government food assistance programs. Philadelphia began offering school lunches in the first decade of the twentieth century, and New York City's Board of Education assumed responsibility for school lunch in the Bronx and Manhattan in 1919.[30] Federal involvement began in the Depression years when the Federal Surplus Commodity Corporation distributed surpluses to schools, a program that continued through World War II. Feeding children in these years, however, was incidental to the primary goals of surplus disposal and employment of people in lunchrooms.[31] After the war, concern over the high number of military draftees who had failed their physical exams because of nutritional deficiencies led Congress to establish a permanent federal lunch program with the passage of the National School Lunch Act of 1946 (NSLA). Section 2 of that act makes clear its multiple purposes: "It is hereby declared to be the policy of Congress, as a measure of national security, to safeguard the health and well-being of the nation's children and to encourage the domestic consumption of nutritious agricultural commodities and other food, by assisting the States [to establish and maintain] school lunch programs."

This second largest of the federal food assistance programs provides a fixed cash reimbursement to schools for each meal, plus a small subsidy (funds from section 4 of the NSLA) to support the labor and equipment necessary to provide cooked meals. In addition, USDA supplies commodities, both specially purchased and from surplus reserves, to augment foods bought by the schools. Administrative costs are largely covered by state matching grants. The program served more than 25 million children in 1996 in more than 93,600 public and private schools at a cost of more than $6 billion.[32]

The program is accessible to all children, although lunch is free only to children from families with incomes at or below 125 percent of the poverty line and at a reduced price to those with family incomes between 125 and 185 percent of the poverty line. Other children pay full price. Roughly half of all lunches were served free in 1996, and another 7 percent were provided at reduced rates.

Federally supported school breakfasts have a briefer history. The origin of this program lies in Lyndon Johnson's Task Force on Agriculture and Rural Life, which recommended in 1965 that the nation establish both a breakfast and a summer feeding program as extensions of school lunch.[33] The administration balked, however, at the cost of initiating two new permanent programs; instead the president agreed to set up a two-year pilot breakfast program. This was authorized, then, in the Child Nutrition Act of 1966. School breakfasts were given permanent authorization for appropriations in 1975.

Many fewer schools and children take part in the school breakfast program, which operates much like the lunch program. A concerted congressional effort begun in 1989 to increase school participation by offering school breakfast start-up grants succeeded in increasing the proportion of schools participating in breakfast from less than half of those that were offering the lunch program to two-thirds by 1996.[34] Still, only 6.3 million children were eating breakfast at school in that year, compared with the nearly 25 million who participated in the lunch program.

A third school food program is special milk, begun in the depression as a way to absorb surplus production. For most of the program's history all children received free or reduced-price milk. As part of the Omnibus Budget Reconciliation Act of 1981, the opening gambit of the Reagan revolution, Congress cut most of the child nutrition programs. The administration sought unsuccessfully to eliminate the school milk program entirely, but Congress chose instead to limit the program just to those schools that do not participate in the federal lunch or breakfast programs, since both of the latter include milk with meals.

The school lunch program took the largest blow in dollar terms in the Reagan budget cuts and had not fully regained its 1980 peak in constant dollar terms even by the mid-1990s. The Reagan White House justified these cuts in part on the grounds that the school feeding programs subsidized the meals of non-poor children. Eliminating the middle-class subsidy was supposed to target the programs more effectively to the needy. To end the subsidy, the administration asked Congress to eliminate the section 4 grants for infrastructure costs, reduce the per-meal reimbursement rate for both breakfast and lunch, and lower the income cutoff for free and reduced-price meals. Congress agreed to the two latter changes, and though it refused to eliminate the section 4 funds entirely, it reduced them by 30 percent.[35]

Shortly after the cuts went into effect, the Senate Agriculture Committee asked GAO to assess the impacts on school lunch participation. The investigation found that with the reduction of the labor and equipment subsidy, nearly 3,000 of the 94,300 schools in the program had decided to drop out, depriving both middle-class and poor children of federally sponsored school lunches.[36] The other changes also affected participation by poor children. Data on individual lunch participation before and after the Omnibus Budget Reconciliation Act of 1981 are shown in table 5-2. About one-third of the children who left the program had been receiving free or reduced-price lunches.[37] Although GAO indicates that participation of children receiving

Table 5-2. *School Lunch Participation before and after the Reagan Budget Cuts, 1979 and 1983*
Students in millions

Payment status	1979	1983
Paying full price	15.3	11.2
Paying reduced price	1.7	1.6
Receiving free lunch	10.0	10.3
Total	27.0	23.1

Source: General Accounting Office, *Participation in the National School Lunch Program*, Report to the Chairman, Senate Committee on Agriculture, Nutrition, and Forestry (Government Printing Office, March 20, 1984), p. 19.

free lunches increased by 3 percent, the report also notes that during the economic recession in these years, the number of families with school-age children with incomes less than 130 percent of the poverty line was increasing by 27.5 percent. The number of children who ate reduced-price lunches fell slightly, but their income group—those families with children making between 130 and 185 percent of the poverty line—increased by 7.6 percent.[38] With the lower income standards, approximately half a million children who had received free meals would now have to pay 40 cents for lunch, while about 450,000 children who had paid 20 cents would now pay 75 cents for lunch.[39]

Each year until 1988 the Reagan and Bush administrations sought the elimination of section 4 funds, but Congress resisted. Some in Congress also sought each year to restore the cuts, but these efforts were unsuccessful. In 1986 they did exempt the child nutrition programs from further cuts that would automatically occur whenever federal deficit targets were not met.

The sharp drop in school lunch funding and its very gradual recovery are more clearly related to political considerations than to assessments of the effectiveness of this program. The important assessments of school lunch, all strongly positive, appeared after the Reagan cuts. The cuts by Congress, then, were a response to the president acting on what he believed to be the strong election mandate of 1980 to reduce the scope of federal spending. The cuts were not a product of congressional skepticism about the value of the lunch program. Nevertheless, subsequent evaluation studies certainly appear to have supported and encouraged congressional attempts to restore the program to its pre-Reagan strength and to maintain it in the 1990s.

Three important evaluations of school lunch and breakfast were sponsored by USDA: the National Evaluation of School Nutrition Programs (1983), the Child Nutrition Program Study (1991 and 1992), and the School Nutrition Dietary Assessment (1993).[40] The findings in each are similar: participants in both school lunch and school breakfast programs had higher nutrient intake and better quality food than children who did not take part; a higher proportion of children eligible for free meals took advantage of the programs than of children eligible for reduced-price meals; and families in the program did not reduce their food expenditures. The 1993 study, conducted by Mathematica for USDA, found that 79 percent of children eligible for free meals participated, as did 71 percent of those who could eat for a reduced price.[41] Although these participation rates are higher than for most federal food assistance programs, they nevertheless mean that between 5 million and 7 million school children who could be eating free or heavily subsidized meals at school are not doing so.

The Child Care Program and Summer Food Service

These two programs have traced radically different funding patterns since the beginning of the Reagan presidency. The child care food program was the fastest growing of all the child nutrition programs, reflecting the rapid growth in the day care industry nationally.[42] The summer food service program, however, saw its funding plunge in response to reports of apparent mismanagement and abuse in the 1970s; it barely survived efforts by the Reagan administration to terminate it altogether. Both programs were established as a single pilot initiative in the 1968 amendments to the National School Lunch Act. They were split into two separate programs in 1975. The child care program provides grants to states to reimburse expenditures for meals served in day care centers.[43] The program is more targeted to the needy than are other child nutrition programs: more than 80 percent of the meals are provided free to children in day care facilities. Summer food service provides free meals during summer vacation to any child living in areas where at least half the children come from families with incomes at or below 185 percent of the poverty line. Neither program seems to have been evaluated to the degree to which school lunch or breakfast have been, but a USDA study of the child care food program did conclude that participating children got nutritionally better food and greater variety than children in day care centers not in the program. Only 60 percent of the nation's day care centers participate.[44]

With a total cost of about $209 million in 1980, summer food service was (and still is) one of the smaller food assistance programs.[45] Yet unlike the significantly larger child care program, which cost more than twice as much in 1980, summer food achieved a degree of visibility out of proportion to its budgetary importance. News of mismanagement and abuse made it a ready symbol of what was wrong with the American welfare state for those interests seeking to reduce the size of the federal government.

In the mid-1970s about three-quarters of the summer food sponsors were private nonprofit groups, such as churches and neighborhood organizations. The remainder were schools and other public agencies, such as parks departments and municipal recreation programs. Many of the nonprofit organizations were clearly unequipped to meet the stringent and often complex requirements for providing meals to children during the summer vacation. Rumors of abuse grew, and Congress asked GAO to investigate.

In its review of the 1976 summer program, GAO found much to be concerned about: many organizations wasted food because they had no refrigeration; rules were broken (some food intended for children was eaten by adults, and meals were consumed off-site, particularly in bad weather at sites with no shelter); some sponsors ordered more meals than demand warranted; and in a few cases, there was evidence of kickbacks by vendors seeking to supply meals to sponsors.[46] GAO recommended limiting sponsorship to schools and nonprofit residential camps, a step Congress did not immediately take.

The following summer GAO visited seventy-five sites in three cities to gauge better the extent of these problems. They found that though some remained, many of the most flagrant abuses were no longer present.[47] When President Reagan took office, however, the administration recommended summer feeding, along with school milk, for termination. Although Congress chose not to accede to the recommendation, the Omnibus Budget Reconciliation Act of 1981 prohibited most nonprofit organizations from serving as sponsors. Ironically, a later congressional study concluded that most of the program abuses had already ended by this date.[48] The impact on the program of the removal of the nonprofit organizations was severe: the program lost about 30 percent of its sponsors, and the number of children served dropped from 1.9 million to 1.4 million between the summers of

1981 and 1982.[49] It took more than a decade for the program to rebuild its client base to its 1981 level.

Commodity Assistance

The federal government currently distributes actual foodstuffs to individuals, soup kitchens, food banks, and other charitable institutions. One small program involves the provision of commodities to American Indians living on reservations. Assistance comes in the form of a monthly commodity food package of fifty or seventy-five pounds. Food distribution on reservations is a sensible alternative to food stamps, for the retail food stores where stamps might be redeemed are a rarity in these locales.

The major commodity program, now called the emergency food assistance program, is reminiscent of Depression-era food distribution efforts. It began in 1981 under a different name with what was to be a one-time-only release of 30 million pounds of surplus cheese to individuals. According to Michael Lipsky and Marc Thibodeau, the text of President Reagan's executive order releasing the cheese made it clear that the primary goal was to reduce the costs to the federal government of storing the surplus. Feeding the hungry was secondary.[50] This special dairy distribution program was replaced in 1983 by the temporary emergency food assistance program (TEFAP), which broadened the types of commodities available for distribution and extended eligibilty from individuals to charitable feeding institutions.

TEFAP was supposed to terminate at the end of six months, but it was extended through September 1985. Since then it has been reauthorized in the Food Security Act of 1985, the Stewart B. McKinney Homeless Assistance Act of 1987, the Hunger Prevention Act of 1988, and the 1990 Food, Agriculture, Conservation, and Trade Act. In the 1990 legislation it quietly lost the word "temporary" from its title, although it is still called by its original acronym. The Personal Responsibility and Work Opportunity Reconciliation Act of 1996 merged TEFAP with the food distribution program to soup kitchens and food banks, which had existed as a separate program only since 1989.

More than any other federal food assistance program, commodity distribution has been reliant to a significant extent on a network of volunteers and nonprofit organizations. Once a state gets its allocation of commodities, it is responsible for coordinating the flow of food to local distribution sites. Although county welfare offices are common conduits, others are religious institutions, nonprofit food pantries, and civic organizations.[51] TEFAP initially distributed only surplus commodities, but during the 1980s federal stockpiles began to diminish. Of the various outlets for federal surplus foods, including the school lunch program and foreign exports, TEFAP was last in priority. Thus to supplement TEFAP stocks, USDA was authorized in 1988 to buy commodities for distribution. Gradually the amount of purchased food overtook and then surpassed the amount of surplus food. In 1995 the only surplus distributed was butter. By 1996 purchased foodstuffs had entirely replaced surpluses, but the total quantity of commodities distributed had fallen to 86 million pounds from a 1987 peak of slightly more than 1 billion pounds. Federal funding to defray states' administrative costs fell from $50 million annually in the period 1983–91 to $40 million in 1995. These declines occurred during a period when demand on food banks and soup kitchens was growing substantially.[52]

Commodity assistance is said to complement food stamps in two ways: First, like WIC, it serves population groups that do not or cannot participate in other food assistance programs, in this case rural dwellers without easy access to grocery stores and a small, primarily elderly population too proud or too overwhelmed by the application process to enroll in the food stamp program. Second, it relies on the local volunteers and charitable organizations that distribute the food to identify needy individuals and alert them to their eligibility for food stamps and other government social services.[53]

A survey of TEFAP recipients conducted in 1986 found that more than 40 percent of recipient households were headed by a person sixty years or older, compared with only 15 percent of food stamp households. Although about 90 percent of TEFAP recipients are eligible for food stamps, only 40 percent are actually enrolled in the latter program, according to one estimate.[54] As a witness from a social service agency commented at a congressional hearing, "Elderly people have claimed the TEFAP program as their own."[55] Like the commodity distribution to Indians living on remote reservation lands, TEFAP fills a niche that food stamps pass over.

Food Assistance as Block Grants

In 1995 the Republican majority in the House of Representatives sought to consolidate the child and maternal nutrition programs into two block grants, passing control over these federal efforts entirely to the respective states. The proposal, part of the Contract With America on which House Republicans ran in 1994, was not designed in response to the perception that the system of food assistance was too fragmented. It was instead part of a larger attempt to refashion the entire welfare system and reduce federal social spending.

Many people regarded the proposals to create nutrition block grants as a severe threat to their effectiveness. That such a threat should come from Congress was unusual. Although there have always been unsympathetic interests in Congress that sought to encumber the food assistance programs with complex and burdensome regulations and that favored cutting appropriations, Congress has for the most part been the champion of food assistance programs in the face of frequent executive skepticism. Only in the first flush of the Reagan revolution had Congress acquiesced to administration desires to cut food assistance.

Early in 1995, fresh from their victory in the midterm elections, House Republicans proposed the creation of a Family Nutrition Block Grant, encompassing WIC and aspects of the child and adult care food program, and a School-based Nutrition Block Grant, consolidating all of the child nutrition programs. Republican members of the House Agriculture Committee, including Bill Emerson of Missouri, did not embrace the proposal, but the Republican majority nevertheless was successful in passing a broad welfare reform bill that contained these block grants. A similar bill was then introduced in the Senate.

For the better part of the year, House and Senate Republicans were at odds over the nutrition block grants. Senate opposition was led by Richard Lugar (R-Ind.), chair of the Senate Agriculture Committee, who was firmly committed to federal control of the school lunch program. In the end, when the bill passed and ultimately emerged from the conference committee, the Senate position had prevailed.

Although the president vetoed that welfare reform bill early in 1996, as he had promised to do all along, the debate over the child food programs provided an opportunity to consider the implications of block granting. As proposed, the block grants would have ended the entitlement to breakfast, lunch, summer food, and child care meals. Instead, states would have received a set amount of funding, which would not fluctuate to accommodate shifts in school or day care enrollment or economic changes, all of which change demand for food assistance. Not only would the termination of open-ended entitlement funding end the stimulus to spending in times of recession, it would likely exacerbate interstate inequities as poor people clustered in some states.

None of these features is a necessary concomitant of the block grant form, although historically, capped funding has tended to accompany block grant designs, from the Community Development Block Grant of 1974 to the Reagan era education and health care block grants. However, state administrative flexibility is an inherent feature of block grants. Such flexibility in allocating the block grants and in setting standards would in all likelihood create unequal treatment of poor people across the states.[56]

Understanding the Federal Food Assistance System

The opportunity to think carefully about a block grant alternative to the multiplicity of targeted food assistance programs, many of them funded on an entitlement basis, casts a particularly favorable light on the existing system. The multiplicity of individual targeted programs appears as an unambiguous virtue, a safeguard for interests that might be lost or shortchanged in the competition for a finite pot of resources that a block grant would set into motion. Infants and pregnant women, who require special nutritional supplements; children from economic or family environments in which regular and nutritious feeding cannot be guaranteed, even through the provision of food stamps; rural people too isolated to rely on retail food outlets; and the homeless and transient poor who rely heavily on soup kitchens are all examples of target populations thought to be poorly or unreliably or inadequately served by the universal food stamp program. Furthermore, the entitlement programs among the food assistance initiatives are genuinely flexible in that they may grow and contract with economic and demographic fluctuations. Finally, for many households the targeted programs make up for some of the inadequacies of the broad food stamp program.

If the design of the targeted programs makes sense, however, the implementation process, from funding to the establishment of eligibility to rule-making, has often been problematic. Although the school lunch program manages to serve almost four out of five children eligible for free meals, most of the other food assistance programs serve much smaller fractions of their target populations. Support for outreach programs, however, is minimal. In addition, Congress has resisted transforming WIC into an entitlement program, thus limiting its clientele to what can be accommodated by annual budgetary appropriations. Commodity distribution has withered in the 1990s, and eligibility and reimbursement rates have been cut for school nutrition programs. All indications are, however, that significant numbers of people still need help.

Sometimes several of the food assistance programs have seemed to function as surrogates in a larger conflict where the issues had little to do directly with feeding the needy. This was true of the contest in the 1970s over the implementation of WIC and during the 1980s, when Republican presidential administrations sought to cut or eliminate the child nutrition programs as part of the effort to dismantle federal domestic initiatives. It is not difficult to argue, finally, that the combination of these targeted programs and the broad food stamp entitlement could decisively end food insecurity, but the potential has simply never been realized.

6 | *Hunger on the Congressional Agenda*

U ntil the late 1960s debates over public food assistance to the needy were almost never framed solely as a problem of hunger in the United States. Instead, food assistance was invariably discussed in the context of agricultural price policy: even some of those members of Congress concerned with the welfare aspects of food aid found it useful to argue that increasing food assistance to the needy would increase demand, absorb the overproduction of farm commodities, and maintain prices.[1] It would be incorrect to suggest that the hungry were merely incidental beneficiaries of these macroeconomic efforts to support the farm economy, but it is certainly the case that their interests were rarely disentangled from those of producer groups as Congress went about constructing the basic programs of federal food assistance.

When domestic hunger emerged on the national scene as a welfare issue, set against the backdrop of the civil rights movement and the War on Poverty, congressional discussion of food assistance programs was no longer framed in the context of agricultural price support policy. In the decades since then, hunger and its policy antidotes have remained in their own right on the congressional political agenda. But the story of congressional interest in this problem is complicated: for the better part of two decades hunger policy was the concern primarily of select committees, not standing committees. These common temporary legislative devices were effective as means of gaining attention for the issue, but they turned out to be weak institutional and political actors for mobilizing national resources over the long term.

Getting on the National Political Agenda

Federal food assistance to the needy had been on the postwar congressional agenda since the early 1950s. Thus when the House was debating legislation to establish a permanent food stamp program in 1964, Leonor Sullivan was able to claim, "I have been living with this issue for 10 years."[2] But it is important to understand that Representative Sullivan's persistence in pursuit of food stamps established a place for a particular program on the congressional agenda, not the problem of hunger itself. Hunger, with all of its powerful emotional freight, arrived on the national scene by a different and more publicly visible route.

Students of the agenda-setting process agree that in certain instances crises or other dramatic events provide the first, catalytic step in the process of transforming a problem into a publicly salient issue.[3] Such "focusing events," as John Kingdon calls them, then typically require powerful policy entrepreneurs to sustain the issue on the political agenda, but the events themselves may nevertheless serve to capture the attention of the public and political decisionmakers.

Jeffrey Berry's account of how hunger appeared on the political agenda closely conforms to this model.[4] As Berry observes, in 1966 domestic hunger was not an issue; by 1967 it had become a matter of public interest and concern. The first date is important, for it suggests that the hunger issue was no mere epiphenomenon of poverty or poverty policy: the War on Poverty had been going on for two years without making the issue of serious food deprivation a central focus.[5] Nor had hunger entered the policy lexicon via the food stamp program, enacted at last into law in 1964. What transformed hunger from a problem to an issue in its own right was the series of dramatic field investigations and reports of malnutrition that occurred in 1967 and 1968.

First came the visit to the Mississippi Delta in April 1967 by the Senate Subcommittee on Employment, Manpower, and Poverty. The subcommittee had originally gone to Jackson, Mississippi, to conduct hearings as part of its routine oversight of the programs of the War on Poverty.[6] Members were reportedly taken by surprise, however, when the testimony was dominated by reports of hunger and starvation, prompting two of their number, Senators Robert Kennedy (D-N.Y.) and Joseph Clark (D-Pa.), to travel into the countryside the next day to observe conditions firsthand.

Closely following on the heels of the Senate visit came the team of doctors, funded by the Field Foundation, to look at hunger among children in rural Mississippi. Their graphic testimony—of listless children who lived on nothing but grits, bread, and Kool-Aid—before the Senate subcommittee that July attracted wide media attention.[7] Then in the spring of 1968 the Citizens' Board of Inquiry published its *Hunger, U.S.A.* report, documenting hunger not only in the delta but on Indian reservations, in Appalachia, and in southwestern barrios. Almost simultaneously a coalition of women's, business, civic, and church groups released "Their Daily Bread," a strong critique of the school lunch program, which found that only about one-third of the 6 million eligible children were receiving free or low-cost lunches. Finally, toward the end of May CBS television broadcast its exposé, "Hunger in America."

However much the scope of hunger was open to debate, its existence at least could not now be ignored. Ardith Maney's detailed examination of the politics of food assistance captures this transformation from problem to public issue in one telling observation: that the debate at this moment in the Johnson administration over how to respond to the building evidence of domestic hunger marked the first time that food assistance policy was discussed in the executive branch without linking it to farm policy. "After 1968," she writes, "there was no going back."[8]

Dramatic revelations, Roger Cobb and Charles Elder suggest, may attract public attention, but they are rarely sufficient to sustain an issue on the political agenda.[9] The issue needs a champion, an effective advocate, or in Kingdon's terms, a policy entrepreneur, someone who invests the issue with legitimacy, helps to define the problem in comprehensible terms, and promotes solutions.[10] If Leonor Sullivan performed this entrepreneurial function for food stamps, it was Robert Kennedy who did so for hunger. As one USDA official observed, "The big change came when Bobby Kennedy got into the act."[11]

Although Kennedy had gone to Mississippi along with Senators Clark, Javits, and George Murphy, it was his visit to delta shacks ("the worst places I've ever seen," according to Charles Evers, the Mississippi civil rights leader who accompanied him) that caught the attention of the news media. "My God," Kennedy is reported to have said as he sat with a desperately hungry child, "I didn't know this kind of thing existed. How can a country like this allow it? *Maybe they just don't know.*"[12] When the subcommittee members returned to Washington, Kennedy and Clark went personally to appeal to Agriculture Secretary Orville Freeman to mount an emergency food program for Mississippi. Seeking presidential support, the entire subcommittee wrote to Lyndon Johnson that they had observed firsthand "conditions of malnutrition and widespread hunger . . . that can only be described as shocking."[13] But then, as the ghetto disorders of the summer of 1967 began to build, Kennedy's focus as "tribune of the underclass" shifted from the problems of the rural South to those of the urban North.[14] Kennedy's role as a hunger advocate seemed to evaporate; by the spring of 1968, when he began actively to pursue the presidency, it was on an altogether different platform. Others, however, were ready to take on the entrepreneurial role.

The Senate Select Committee

Since the dramatic reports of 1967–68, the task of keeping the problem of hunger in the public eye and on the formal Washington agenda has primarily fallen to three sets of lead actors: the Senate Select Committee on Nutrition and Human Needs, the House Select Committee on Hunger, and an informal coalition of private voluntary advocacy organizations. Since the House select committee and most of the advocacy groups were not established until the 1980s, the first institutional actor of importance was the Senate select committee, which defined and dominated the debate for almost a full decade. Under the leadership of George McGovern (D-S.D.), this body set out to study domestic hunger and its consequences and to promote a multifaceted federal response.

The story of the Senate select committee is a paradoxical one: although it can claim to have greatly expanded the nation's understanding of hunger and to have stimulated major additions and changes in the system of federal food assistance, it is also to a certain extent a study in marginality by virtue of its institutional limitations. Select committees, in contrast to the standing committees of Congress, are typically established as investigative bodies whose purpose is to make recommendations on some specific problem to their full house. They are not allowed, however, to report legislation to the floor. Furthermore, they usually operate on a year-to-year basis, obliging them to defend annually not only their budget request but their very existence. Although recent history affords a few examples of select committees that wielded significant power, William Morrow argues that their funda-mental weakness is their "lack of legislative status within the committee sys-tem [that] has forced these committees to the periphery of interest both from within Congress and from outside pressure group interests."[15]

For nearly nine years, from 1968 through the end of 1977, the Senate Select Committee on Nutrition and Human Needs confronted and to some extent overcame these weaknesses. At least three aspects of the Senate select committee are of interest here: its self-conscious assumption of an agenda-setting role, its gradual (though short-lived) institutionalization as the national hunger conscience, and its roster of accomplishments.

The establishment of the Senate select committee had been a direct response to the private studies of hunger released in the spring of 1968.[16] Its formal mandate was ambitious: to study the food, medical, and other related needs of the people of the United States and propose to the Senate the sort of coordinated program that would provide these basic necessities to everyone. All this was to be completed within a year, at which time the select committee would go out of business.

Members of the committee believed that it was their role to spread the news of hunger, not only to their colleagues in the Senate but to the gov-ernment and the nation at large. Convinced already that hunger was wide-spread, the committee nevertheless understood that there were doubters, that its members confronted, in the words of Agriculture Secretary Freeman, the "rocky soil of public indifference, watered with often casual interest of the Congress, State legislatures and local units of government."[17] But Senator Walter Mondale (D-Minn.) was sure that an informed public would provide the crucial catalyst for action, and it was the select commit-tee's function to provide that education. Just as Robert Kennedy had implied the year before, sitting in a delta shack, the key, in Mondale's view, depended on *making people know*: "the public will act to force its govern-ment to eliminate hunger when it knows the magnitude and depth of the tragedy."[18] Senator Jacob Javits (R-N.Y.) was also convinced of the impor-tance of information, in this case for his own colleagues in the Senate: "We have to prove these things. We do not expect the Senate to take it on faith. . . . We have to prove the facts."[19] To get hunger to a central place on the agenda, the Senate select committee had to educate both the public and the government.

To do this it set out as its first order of business, as we saw in chapter 3, the establishment of some sort of hunger count. The committee was deter-mined to offer a hard indicator of the scope of the problem, no matter how flawed. In his study of agenda setting, Kingdon stresses the important role of measurement. "The countable problem," he writes, "sometimes acquires a power of its own that is unmatched by problems that are less countable."[20] Quantification is a way of substantiating the claim that there is a problem and thus opens the way to move the problem to the political agenda. As McGovern explained,

> Prominent and prestigious Members of the House said in effect there is no starvation or malnutrition in the United States. We who felt that action should be taken were not in a position to successfully contradict them because we did not have the facts. We had not made the kind of thoughtful, systematic investigation that this committee is now in the process of making.[21]

The Senate initially voted to establish the select committee for a five-month period through the end of 1968. Then it extended the life of the committee for another year. But it was clear immediately that the committee could not accomplish its agenda in so short a time, and its leaders returned to the Senate to ask for an additional extension.[22] Opponents, most of them southern Democrats, worried that the select committee was not only overstepping its original mandate but that it would become a fixture.[23] "There is nothing more permanent than one of these temporary committees," Senator Allen Ellender (D-La.) complained in the debate over extending the select committee for a third year.[24]

Nevertheless, the select committee continued to win annual extensions through 1977. During that time, its role shifted from that of a primarily educative body dedicated to calling attention to the existence of domestic hunger to that of the major institutional shaper of food assistance policy. In this role the select committee emerged as an oversight vehicle and as the most visible advocate for the hungry. In addition, McGovern sought to broaden the scope of the committee's concerns beyond hunger and its roots in poverty. Beginning in 1974, he held hearings on fashioning a national nutrition policy, which he viewed as encompassing the development of national nutrition standards, nutrition education, and a federal policy on food additives. The result of the select committee's annual extension and the expansion of its interests beyond the special investigative and educational tasks for which it had been established was to create, for all intents and purposes, a de facto standing subcommittee.

The extensions of the select committee's life and the broadening of its functions were accomplished by the timely exploitation of various events, revelations, and crises in the hunger arena. How could one think of terminating the select committee, the argument went, when there was such compelling evidence of its necessity? In arguing for the first annual extension, for example, Javits took the position that the just-completed White House Conference on Food, Nutrition, and Health required extensive follow-up studies, a job the select committee was well qualified to do.[25] A year later, the select committee's advocates argued for another extension on the grounds that the president's promise that every poor child would be receiving a free or reduced-price lunch by Thanksgiving 1970 had just been shown to have fallen far short. The select committee was the natural body to investigate the shortfall in participation. During yet another debate over extension, McGovern suggested that if it had not been for the select committee's vigilance, 2 million people would have been eliminated from the food stamp rolls by virtue of a change in eligibility standards. The select committee had managed to block implementation of the new standards. At the same time an alert select committee discovered that the summer recreation feeding program for children was underfunded; members succeeded in tripling the appropriation. Arguing for another extension in March 1974, McGovern claimed that the select committee was in a unique position to offer leadership "in one of the most serious crises the Nation has ever faced. I am speaking, of course, of the general food crisis we have been experiencing for over a year now."[26] Clearly, the general argument went, the food assistance programs required constant monitoring, and the select committee was the vehicle to provide this oversight.

In its role as de facto standing subcommittee on hunger and food assistance, the select committee was more than a watchdog body responding to perceived crises and challenges. It also served as the clearinghouse for information on the routine functioning of federal food assistance programs and their reform and modification. In its brief life it held countless hearings on such subjects as the effectiveness of the commodity distribution program, the effects of food stamp regulations on participation rates, nutritional needs of older Americans and children of migrant laborers, and nutrition education. In addition to its watchdog and clearinghouse roles, the committee's small staff participated actively in drafting legislation to modify the food stamp program and the Nutrition Education Act of 1975, and committee members played key roles in the passage over President Ford's veto of the Child Nutrition and School Lunch Act. Thus even on the very eve of its termination, the Senate Select Committee on Nutrition and Human Needs seemed institutionalized as the key congressional actor in the hunger and food assistance field. Apparently unaware of its coming demise, a select committee document requesting extension through 1977 summed up its prior year's activities and then noted that "rather than appearing to near the end of the need for such a Committee at any point, consistently the demands for its role have expanded beyond its resources. . . . During the Second Session of the 94th Congress, the Committee staff will . . . develop specific recommendations for the longer term."[27]

The termination of the select committee was the product of a Senate effort to reform a committee system whose growth and elaboration was seen by many as out of control. One way to rationalize the system was to eliminate most of the thirty-four special committees, joint committees, and select committees.[28] In the inevitable bargaining and backing and filling that eventuated from the reform proposal to wipe out these various temporary committees, a number were exempted from termination, including ones concerning small business, veterans, aging, Indian affairs, and intelligence. The Select Committee on Nutrition and Human Needs, however, was to be disbanded; in its place there would be a new Subcommittee on Nutrition in the newly expanded standing Senate Committee on Agriculture, Nutrition, and Forestry.

McGovern led a bipartisan fight to include the Select Committee on Nutrition and Human Needs among the exempted. Not only was its work not done, its proponents argued, but to enfold the select committee in the Agriculture Committee was, in the words of the *New York Times*, close to "sending the chickens off to live with the foxes."[29] Or as Senator Robert Dole (R-Kan.), an ally of McGovern's in this matter, argued, "The Nutrition Committee deals with topics in too much depth to risk its assimilation—and dissimilation—in the Agriculture and Forestry Committee."[30] Nevertheless, the whole Senate was unmoved, either by McGovern's plea to save the select committee entirely or by a compromise he then offered simply to extend its life for two more years.

Despite its bipartisan composition and its respected membership, the Senate Select Committee on Nutrition and Human Needs was simply too weak politically, both inside and outside the Senate, to survive. Skepticism and even outright opposition by members from the South had been a constant over the life of the select committee, and many on the Agriculture Committee had always been concerned about jurisdictional infringement.[31] Reflecting on the history of the select committee, Senator Charles Percy (R-Ill.), a member from the beginning, commented, "I do not know of another committee which has had to come before the Congress every single year and give a report card on everything it has done; which had to lay bare its whole soul and have an accountability to the whole Senate, as we have had year after year after year."[32]

Other Senate partisans of the select committee were convinced that the hunger committee died because it lacked external clout. "It is a sad commentary upon the Senate," noted Senator Edward Brooke (R-Mass.), "if a committee needed by so many was abolished largely because its constituency was mostly poor or disorganized and thus unable to bring pressure to bear upon Congress as effectively as more powerful interest groups."[33] In the end, the Senate agreed to allow the select committee to finish out the calendar year 1977 before transferring its functions to the Agriculture Committee.

The termination of the Senate select committee coincided with legislation in 1977 eliminating the purchase price of food stamps, a major victory for those who argued that even the most minimal cash outlay was beyond the means of the poorest of the poor. Although issues remained to be resolved—how to deal with a spending cap for food stamps that Congress had just imposed and how to combat hunger among migrant workers and Indians—there was a sense that the conquest of domestic hunger was in view. Writing of this moment in the history of food assistance programs, Berry concluded that "of all the major poverty-related problems that the federal government attacked during the 1960s, hunger probably came the closest to being solved."[34]

Hearings conducted in 1979 by McGovern's new Subcommittee on Nutrition encouraged this view. The purpose of the hearings was to reconvene many of those who a decade earlier had called the nation's attention to hunger in Mississippi and Appalachia. Some of these witnesses had actually gone back to the South in 1977 under the auspices of the Field Foundation to examine progress in the struggle against hunger, and they came away convinced that there had been significant gains. Summarizing their testimony, McGovern noted at the hearings that "ten years after we began our efforts, millions of Americans are better off; poverty-caused malnutrition has been reduced. Poverty is still a fact of life, but in the area of food, there is a difference. . . . The Nation's nutrition programs work."[35]

As the sense of crisis receded, no single institution or organization emerged to replace the Senate select committee in keeping hunger on the national agenda. In what appears to have been an attempt to pass responsibility in this domain to the executive branch, both houses of Congress passed resolutions in 1977 urging the president to establish a commission on domestic and international hunger and malnutrition, to be funded, not by Congress, but by White House discretionary monies.[36] Although some part of the mission of this new executive branch body would be to study domestic hunger, the main purpose was to seek ways to reduce hunger in the rest of the world.[37] President Carter had in fact already appointed an interagency task force, the White House World Hunger Study Group, to examine U.S. food and agriculture programs and policies as they bore on international hunger. In the early fall of 1978, apparently in response to Congress, Carter transformed the study group into a Presidential Commission on World Hunger.[38] When Carter's commission finally issued its report in March 1980, however, it did little to advance an understanding of domestic hunger: only 15 of its 251 pages were devoted to hunger in the United States, which the authors suggested was a problem mainly for migrant workers, Indians, and the elderly poor.[39]

The House Select Committee

Hunger in the United States reappeared in a more prominent place on the national political agenda in the early 1980s and was sustained there for a decade in much the same way the process had occurred in the late 1960s. A series of reports by various advocacy and local government groups outside of Washington galvanized Congress—this time the House of Representatives rather than the Senate—to assume responsibility for highlighting and addressing hunger issues. This is the context in which the House Select Committee on Hunger was born. Indeed, the lifespan of its history, from its origins to its demise, is strikingly similar to that of the Senate select committee. Like its Senate counterpart, the House select committee functioned for about nine years educating the public and government and articulating solutions. But also like its Senate counterpart, the House select committee operated outside the framework of the standing committee system and thus lacked essential authority. In 1993 it was allowed to expire, the victim of a budget-cutting measure.

The reemergence of concern over hunger was the product of the two-year recession that began in 1981. Yet even as the national unemployment rate was approaching 11 percent, the first Reagan budget was tightening food stamp eligibility standards and cutting food aid appropriations. Although the number of people below the federal poverty line rose from 31.8 million in 1981 to 35.3 million in 1983, the number of people receiving food stamps in the average month actually fell by more than 800,000.[40] In 1982 the U.S. Conference of Mayors reported sharp increases in demand for food pantry services, a trend that was confirmed by more than a dozen subsequent studies by groups that ranged from the National Council of Churches to Bread for the World to the Harvard School of Public Health.[41]

Alarmed at these reports of growing hunger in the United States and galvanized as well by a famine in the Horn of Africa, Representatives Mickey Leland (D-Tex.) and Ben Gilman (R-N.Y.) offered a resolution in 1983 to create a House Select Committee on Hunger. Opponents of a new select committee argued that its establishment would fragment congressional efforts in the hunger fight, but its sponsors pointed out that at least eight standing committees already had some jurisdiction over various aspects of food assistance policy. Curiously, the experience and even the existence of the Senate Select Committee on Nutrition and Human Needs, an obvious reference point, were never mentioned in the House debate. The full House passed the Leland-Gilman resolution overwhelmingly in 1984, and every two years thereafter through the 1992 session it voted to reconstitute the select committee. Gilman's interest was chiefly in international hunger issues, but Leland, the principal source of the idea for a select committee, was impelled by his observation of hunger in his own home district.[42] In his remarks in support of the resolution establishing the select committee, Leland cited data on the rise of hunger in Houston, but then went on to point out that similar reports were coming from states and cities in all regions across the country.[43] Tony Hall (D-Ohio), who succeeded Leland as chair of the select committee when Leland was killed in an airplane crash in Africa in 1989, was concerned with both international and domestic hunger. He had been a Peace Corps volunteer in Thailand in the 1960s, and he had seen hungry children in Ethiopia in the early 1980s. The experience had deeply troubled him.[44] Back home he had persuaded a Dayton grocery magnate to conduct a hunger survey in the city, which found that demand for food pantry services had doubled in the year.[45] In the debate over the formation of the select committee, Hall took pains to suggest that his district was not unique, citing reports of increasing hunger by such advocacy groups as the Food Research and Action Center, the

Center on Budget and Policy Priorities, and the Citizens Commission on Hunger in New England.[46]

The mandate of the House select committee, which could not introduce legislation, was to study hunger issues, review presidential and executive branch recommendations relating to hunger, and recommend legislation to the appropriate committees. Over the course of its life, from the 99th through the 102d Congress, the House select committee held 109 sets of hearings. Reflecting the interests of the principal actors on the committee, the subject matter of these hearings was split almost evenly between international (56) and domestic (53) subjects. Among the latter, the House select committee devoted extensive energies to exploring the barriers to participation in various federal food assistance programs.

It also promoted two pieces of legislation, neither of which made a major impact on the structure of federal food assistance or antipoverty policy. One was the Mickey Leland Childhood Hunger Relief Act, whose object was to provide more generous food stamp benefits to families with children. First introduced in 1990, the act finally passed as part of the Omnibus Budget Reconciliation Act of 1993. Touted as "the most important anti-hunger legislation . . . in the last fifteen years," this unprepossessing monument to Leland turned out to be a hodgepodge of modest changes in existing law and programs designed to expand food stamp eligibility among low-income families with children.[47] The second piece of legislation pushed by the House select committee was the Freedom from Want Act, another admixture whose major elements were introduced piecemeal, either as individual bills or as amendments to other bills. These various initiatives had a range of fates. For example, President Bush vetoed an urban aid bill that contained a freedom from want provision that would have allowed AFDC recipients to accumulate up to $10,000 in assets to start a microenterprise. But another element of the bill, one that allows local governments to spend Community Development Block Grant money for microenterprise development, was successfully attached to community development spending legislation as an amendment.

In the early days of the 103d Congress in 1993, the select committee unexpectedly died, the victim of a congressional economy drive. Those who led the effort claimed that the four existing House select committees were a waste of money and that Congress itself had to bear some of the sacrifices that others faced in a period of budget cutting. When the membership voted not to reauthorize the House Select Committee on Narcotics, widely regarded as the select committee with the strongest backing, Democratic

House leaders did not even bring renewal of the hunger select committee to a floor vote. Its authorization simply expired on March 31, 1993.[48]

Chairman Hall did not go quietly. Claiming that the House had lost its conscience, Hall began a three-week fast to protest the demise of his select committee. Religious and lay organizations involved in hunger advocacy rallied to the cause, and President Clinton wrote to Hall praising his "moral leadership on this issue."[49] As Hall ended his fast (having lost twenty-three pounds), the World Bank announced that it would sponsor a conference on international hunger, Secretary of Agriculture Mike Espy pledged to convene a similar gathering on domestic hunger, and the House Democratic leadership pledged to support the formation of a congressional Hunger Caucus, a promise realized that fall.

For a little more than a year the Hunger Caucus served as the focal point in Congress for anti-hunger activities. Technically, this voluntary body, which claimed about seventy members from both parties, was one of twenty-seven so-called legislative service organizations, established to promote and publicize a particular cause or issue in the House. Unlike select committees, which are financed by congressional appropriations, funding of the caucuses came from members' personal office accounts. The function of the Hunger Caucus was to organize briefings, provide hearing support, and serve as an information clearinghouse on hunger issues, though in a larger context the leaders of the Hunger Caucus saw their role as carrying on the agenda-setting function of the defunct select committee by "pushing responsible policies and generating a national sense of urgency to solve hunger once and for all."[50] At the same time, Hall set up a congressional hunger center outside the legislative body altogether, funded entirely by private and foundation funds, to perform a variety of education and coordination tasks.

In the Republican congressional revolution of 1995, the new majority eliminated the caucuses, including the short-lived Hunger Caucus, leaving Hall and the remaining congressional hunger fighters without a governmental foothold. One of the chief consequences in the hunger arena was to shift agenda-setting functions substantially to the voluntary advocacy sector.

The Significance of the House Select Committee

It is perhaps an exaggeration to claim that the House select committee "was . . . the most important voice—and at times, the sole voice—for the poor and hungry of America and the world."[51] But the House Select Committee on Hunger did serve as an important national political forum for raising, defining, and considering hunger issues. Not since the days of McGovern's Senate select committee had any body or actor in this policy domain occupied for so long such an institutionally visible place from which to operate.

In seeking to place and keep hunger issues on the political agenda, the House select committee made three contributions of particular note. One is that it embraced the notion of food security and did much to publicize and legitimate the concept. A second was that it served as a Washington-based forum and coordinator for hunger advocates of all types. A third was that it quickly developed an interest in addressing the underlying causes of hunger rather than focusing on the food assistance programs alone.

The Senate Select Committee on Nutrition and Human Needs had approached hunger issues through the malnutrition lens. McGovern's interest in exploring the notion of a national nutrition policy was a natural extension of the conception of hunger as a problem of malnourishment. The House select committee in contrast viewed hunger in the food security framework. When Hall became chair of the House select committee, he often told people that his objective was to make sure that everyone was able to go into a supermarket and buy food.[52] Access on a regular basis to normal or conventional channels of food supply—grocery stores, farmers' markets, and federal food assistance programs—became the central theme of the select committee's inquiries and reports on domestic hunger.[53]

The select committee's interest in access issues is reflected in countless hearings in which the questions at stake had to do with barriers to participation in federal food assistance programs. The difficulties people faced in taking advantage of programs like WIC and food stamps was an abiding source of concern and frustration for Hall and his colleagues. "Despite this network of programs," the committee observed in what turned out to be its final report, "millions of persons fail to access services for which they are eligible."[54]

Like its predecessor body in the Senate, the House select committee served as a nationally visible forum for a range of hunger advocates and organizations. For nearly a decade, through its hearings in Washington and various regional sites, it provided steady opportunities for publicizing hunger issues. Committee staff people were proud of their ability to offer a platform for a wide range of organizations engaged in the hunger fight: religious and secular groups, corporate foundations and the small food pantry operations, federal food assistance programs, and the county social welfare offices.[55] Committee staff and leaders saw their body as the central node in the organizational network of the hunger advocacy community: the chief convener, catalyst, communicator, and coordinator. Although some of the voluntary groups suggest that the House select committee exaggerated its role,[56] it is certainly the case that Representative Hall worked hard at playing these central functions. After the major national hunger organizations released the Medford Declaration, a statement of intent to end domestic hunger by 1995, Hall and Bill Emerson (the ranking minority member on the committee), sent a letter to all their House colleagues inviting them to join the list of signatories.[57] In its role as "the official conscience of the nation" on the hunger issue, the House select committee also held hearings to build support for the Medford Declaration.[58] "The anti-hunger community is very fragmented," Hall observed. "Hunger advocates devote time and great effort to local problems. . . . But they have never come together to develop a national agenda to build support for hunger initiatives. This is why the Medford Declaration can be so useful. . . . It brings the different fragments of the hunger community together."[59]

The select committee is also important for its emerging interest in a variety of antipoverty programs designed to address the root causes of hunger. Like the Senate body under McGovern's leadership, the House select committee strayed from a strict focus on hunger and food assistance. Whereas McGovern pursued his growing interest in nutrition issues, Hall pushed microenterprise development, individual development accounts, and other means of providing poor people with the resources to establish independence from public aid. Hall believed that there were plenty of organizations devoted to monitoring and expanding federal food assistance programs; while he would support those efforts, he believed that the committee's role should be broader, focusing on, as he called them, asset-based strategies. The result was to expand the scope of the hunger debate.

Conclusions

The experience of the two select committees, one in the Senate, the other in the House, recalls the old adage about municipal reform groups: Tammany philosopher George Washington Plunkitt once likened them to morning glories, blossoming brilliantly early in the day but fading by evening. In short, they had no staying power. Certainly, this was true of the two congressional select committees, particularly compared with the standing committees of

Congress. In part, the explanation for their short lifespan surely lies in the fact that the constituents that the select committees could mobilize—that is, whose support and resources they could count on—were essentially the various nonprofit advocacy organizations, not hungry people themselves, not the producer groups from agriculture or food processing, and not the retail food sector. Given the limited resources of the hunger advocacy community, Congress as a whole could not be made to pay for abolishing the select committees. In this sense, the select committees were weak politically.

The select committee is also an imperfect institutional device for sustaining an issue on the political agenda. It is true that for elevating the issue of domestic hunger to the agenda in the first place, the select committees, blossoming brightly, were effective. They certainly drew more attention over longer periods of time than the various presidential commissions and task forces on hunger, and they clearly helped to shape views, if not among the public then at least among members of Congress, on hunger and food assistance.[60]

The select committees also functioned in the agenda-setting process as institutional vehicles for policy entrepreneurs, dedicated individuals with a sense of mission and programmatic objectives. It is likely that neither Senator McGovern nor Representative Hall could have operated so persistently as such passionate hunger advocates within the confines of the regular committee system. The select committees were the creations of these policy entrepreneurs and operated in response to their agendas.

But both committees were terminated while there was still, by any standard, much work to be done. Hall not only felt that his select committee had a moral claim to reauthorization but that it had acquired de facto standing status: "We're not a legislative committee, yet we produce legislation," he argued in the battle to save the select committees in 1993.[61] But in fact the two hunger select committees lived only from year to year and were finally easy targets of congressional skeptics, budget cutters, and reformers.

7 | *The Anti-Hunger Advocacy Group Network*

With the demise of an institutionalized congressional forum, anti-hunger interests must rely principally on the community of voluntary groups to keep the issue on the political agenda. The landscape of the anti-hunger movement is populated by a multitude of such groups of varying sizes, shapes, and purposes. Some operate as action arms of mainstream churches; others are religious but nondenominational and ecumenical; still others have emerged from the secular political left. A few groups have ties to corporate interests. Yet despite the manifest differences among the various voluntary organizations, it is nonetheless possible to speak of a relatively cohesive anti-hunger movement with a set of common objectives.

These groups are not well endowed financially, but they do purport to represent what is, collectively, a very large constituency of church and synagogue members and lay grassroots activists. Despite their considerable differences, this community of organizations and its component parts have managed to achieve a division of labor and a variety of coordinating mechanisms. Such an arrangement enables them frequently to speak with one voice.

A multiplicity of diverse organizations pursuing the same general goal potentially poses a number of challenges to the ability of the movement to articulate its positions and to bring its collective weight to bear. For one thing, there is competition for resources among these groups. Anti-hunger groups rely heavily on private donations of food and money, and they also depend on volunteer time. All are in finite supply. Then there is the problem of coordination. The issue of coordination is important to the extent that anti-hunger organizations aspire to a political role. If an organization is devoted simply to the delivery of food to the needy, then (since there are more than enough clients to go around) its main concern is to compete with other providers for the available private and government resources. But if a group seeks to influence public policy in the realm of food assistance or the underlying causes of hunger, then it must figure out a way to join with others to articulate a common position.

The problem of coordination for the purpose of influencing the national political agenda is a concern mainly of those associations that self-consciously seek to play some sort of lobbying role. These groups do not wish to work at cross purposes as they lobby Congress or USDA.

Another coordination task is to provide leadership for a vast array of state and local groups. Coordination among the largest organizations becomes particularly important when the anti-hunger movement seeks to mobilize the vast local infrastructure for political purposes. The mobilization of the grassroots groups depends in the first place on the establishment of common goals and a common strategy at the top.

The number of groups that play some role on the national scene in hunger politics is certainly no greater than two dozen; the number of major national actors is less than half that. Nevertheless, even this comparatively manageable total raises problems of coordination for political action, for it is a group notable for its diversity. Agreement on goals and strategies cannot be assumed. Setting the agenda and influencing outcomes are issues that must be worked out within the anti-hunger community before they are contested in the larger political arena.

When first the Senate and then the House select committees were in operation in their respective decades, the various voluntary anti-hunger groups had a clear, sympathetic focus in government.[1] Although lobby groups often worked in unison to communicate with or influence these committees, such self-conscious coordination was not always necessary. The select committees could digest, filter, blend, and adapt the individual messages of the disparate organizations. Out of this welter of communications by the politically active anti-hunger advocates, the select committees were able to assemble and craft the elements of the congressional hunger agenda. Agenda-setting, then, was very plainly an interactive process between Congress and voluntary interest groups of all sorts.

On various occasions anti-hunger organizations had sought ways of coordinating and coalescing with one another well before the termination of the select committees and the defunding of the congressional Hunger Caucus in the 1990s. But the demise of formal congressional focal points created new incentives for the interest groups to work out alternative coordinating devices and strategies to form a pyramid of influence.

The Organized Anti-Hunger Community

The first national voluntary anti-hunger organizations were established in the waning days of the War on Poverty. Before this the key actors outside Congress involved in calling attention to the prevalence of domestic hunger were physicians, such as the Field Foundation team that visited the South in 1967, the news media, and local social service and welfare professionals. Then in 1969 and 1970 the federal Office of Economic Opportunity provided start-up funding for three anti-hunger organizations: the Food Research and Action Center (FRAC), the Children's Foundation, and the Community Nutrition Institute.[2] Each was different in its basic mission, thus establishing what has been a persistent pattern of diversity in the organized hunger community. Subsequent hunger organizations were formed without public funding by national church organizations or coalitions of religious leaders, by community organizers, and by individual philanthropists. The major national anti-hunger organizations and their dates of establishment are listed below.[3]

Food Research and Action Center	1970
Bread for the World	1973
Interfaith Impact for Peace and Justice	1974
World Hunger Year	1975
Second Harvest	1979
RESULTS	1980
Center on Budget and Policy Priorities	1981
Share Our Strength	1984
Tufts Center on Hunger, Poverty and Nutrition Policy	1990

The typical structure consists of an umbrella organization that oversees a number of local groups with varying degrees of independence. For example, Second Harvest oversees 185 private food banks, which in turn supply private food donations and government commodities to more than 41,000 private nonprofit food-providing agencies. Some of these are certified by Second Harvest—that is, monitored on a regular basis—while others are classified simply as affiliates. Catholic Charities USA, another umbrella organization, presides over 1,400 local Roman Catholic social service agencies for whom hunger relief is only one of several major welfare concerns. Foodchain, based in Atlanta, is the national parent organization of yet another coalition of 125 independent local groups that collect and redistribute perishable foods from restaurants and hotels. RESULTS, a grassroots lobbying organization based in Washington, D.C., claims eighty member organizations around the United States.[4] These major national organizations represent just a sampling of the population of similar groups active against hunger.

The list of major groups does not, of course, exhaust the roster of organizational actors in national hunger politics. A number of groups participate actively in hunger coalitions but are too new or too small to claim a position of national prominence. The Evangelical Lutheran Church of America's Washington-based Office of Government Affairs and the small Community Nutrition Institute are good examples. Other organizations, such as the Children's Defense Fund, are involved with a range of issues, of which hunger is only one. Some multi-issue groups, such as the U.S. Catholic Conference, participate with the organized anti-hunger community but prefer to remain at an arm's length.

An examination even of the brief list of major national organizations reveals the complexity of the cleavage lines among the hunger groups. One important distinction is that between the secular and the "faith-based" organizations. Some of the latter are social service or political action arms of particular denominations: the Lutheran Office for Governmental Affairs, Catholic Charities USA, the Presbyterian Hunger Program, and Mazon ("the Jewish response to hunger") are examples. Others are interdenominational, such as Bread for the World, which calls itself a "Christian citizens' lobby," and Interfaith Impact, an ecumenical lobbying organization identified with the prophetic justice movement that includes Jewish and Muslim as well as Christian organizations.[5] For most groups, both secular and religious, the differences are rarely a barrier to coordination. Organization leaders stress their common interests in social justice. "We're all on the same side," the chief lobbyist in the Lutheran Office for Governmental Affairs commented.[6] The only major group that mentioned any difficulties in working across religious lines was the U.S. Catholic Conference. Although the conference Office of Domestic Social Development coordinates occasionally with organizations in the anti-hunger community, Catholic positions on policy issues derive not from interactions within an interest coalition but rather from Catholic teachings and religious doctrine.[7] As the director of the conference office noted, "When we write letters on an issue, we cite specific public policy positions articulated by the bishops. . . . For us to sign on to a letter, we'd have to get layers of review and approval here. So it's easier for us to just write our own letter. We can't be at a meeting with a group of organizations and agree then and there to sign something."[8] Even so, conference spokespersons were able to cite a number of instances in which the U.S. Catholic Conference coordinated with both secular and other religious organizations in particular undertakings.

Another difference in the hunger community is between those organizations that emphasize political action, in the form particularly of lobbying or grassroots mobilization, such as FRAC and Bread for the World, and those committed mainly to delivering food assistance and supporting direct food providers. This difference is a matter of organizational emphasis. Although a few groups determinedly avoid exposure in the political arena, such as Share Our Strength, strict compartmentalization between delivery and support functions and political action is not common.[9] An official at Bread for the World noted that his organization was "working to politicize service organizations and networks. We are pushing Second Harvest to politicize the food banks, and they've been very responsive. Same with Catholic Charities USA: they're much more active politically than they were a few years ago."[10] Foodchain, a group devoted to the collection and distribution of surplus prepared foods, has joined with others to press Congress for food stamp reform. Catholic Charities USA, which runs more than 200 soup kitchens across the country, has taken an active role in Interfaith Impact's Food Policy Working Group, a coalition formed to push for food assistance reform and expansion. By and large the gap between the political advocates and the providers is bridged by the willingness of the latter to accede to the political leadership of the former.

Other fault lines in the hunger community add layers of complexity to the problem of alliance-building and coordination. Some groups, such as RESULTS, are focused more on hunger as an international issue than on domestic hunger. Bread for the World, established in response to the 1973 World Food Conference, alternates international and domestic themes from year to year. Some leaders of groups that focus on domestic hunger consider Bread for the World and RESULTS "important to the U.S. hunger movement but not central to it" by virtue of their interest in world hunger.[11] Bread for the World counters with the view that "we live in a global society."[12]

The key anti-hunger organizations are also divided in their analysis of the most effective response to hunger. Organizations like FRAC and the Tufts Center on Hunger, Poverty and Nutrition Policy believe that government, not private, programs are the answer and that these already exist; they simply need constant monitoring, administrative fine tuning, and full funding to be effective.[13] "Our basic tenet," the director of FRAC commented, "is that we don't need to reinvent food programs. If food stamps, WIC, and others were funded adequately, we'd have a good safety net. The design and coverage are pretty good."[14] The job of the hunger lobby in this view should be to protect and expand the food assistance programs. But many of the church-based anti-hunger groups, as well as Second Harvest and to a degree Share Our Strength, are less inclined to focus on the expansion of public food assistance, seeking rather to facilitate or provide food aid through the voluntary charitable sector.

Other organizations, however, believe that their main priority is to address the root causes of hunger—poverty, political powerlessness, dependence. Fully stocked church food pantries and a fully funded food stamp program are stopgap measures in the fight against hunger. Bread for the World and RESULTS are committed to political education and grassroots mobilization, not just food aid. Many in the root-cause wing of the anti-hunger movement promote the development of microenterprise subsidies to allow poor people to form small business undertakings.[15] Those associated with this position talk of "empowerment" and "teaching people to fish" rather than doling out food itself.

These are not hard and fast divisions, of course. Share Our Strength, which funds food delivery operations, is also interested in supporting "empowerment programs" that go beyond emergency food aid.[16] And FRAC officials acknowledge that food stamps, no matter how generously funded, cannot solve the problem of poverty.[17] But organizational and strategic priorities among the anti-hunger groups may nevertheless be arrayed along a continuum of solutions to hunger that range from government food aid on one end to charitable feeding programs toward the center to political and economic empowerment on the other end.

Transcending Differences

If the high degree of organizational diversity is the most notable feature of the anti-hunger community, its second most salient characteristic has been the ability of its members to transcend their differences in the service of the hunger cause. In part this has been possible because the various groups have managed to keep out of one another's way in areas that might ordinarily lead to friction. William Browne has pointed out that interest groups in the same broad policy domain often follow distinctive paths, seeking out relatively narrow issue niches where they "only infrequently become adversaries."[18] In the anti-hunger community, however, the impulse to carve out distinctive niches extends beyond issue concerns: though these organizations are concerned with the same broad issue of hunger, they exhibit niche behavior by seeking to tap different funding veins, serving different clienteles among the hungry, and pursuing a distinctive set of missions for the community of anti-hunger groups. In addition to the specialization implied by this niche strategy, the ability of the anti-hunger groups to overcome divisions is also the product of a set of deliberate efforts to create coordinating structures.

Niche Behavior

Competition for money represents one of the prime dangers of organizational fragmentation. The hunger issue is not so salient that it engages a vast segment of the money-giving American public; thus the field is characterized at first glance by a variety of supplicants pursuing a relatively small number of donors.[19] Two factors save the anti-hunger organizations from destructive competition. One is that most are very small operations in budgetary terms; the other is that the groups have managed for the most part to seek different sources of financial support.

Budgets for many of the major national anti-hunger organizations are under $1 million per year. Annual revenues range as high as $6.4 million (Share Our Strength), but most bring in much less. Most revenues in organizations like World Hunger Year, Share Our Strength, Foodchain, and

Second Harvest do not go for operations but are given away as grants to local providers. Anti-hunger groups are notable for their lean organizational structures.

To meet their modest needs, most groups have identified funding sources that they do not have to share. The various church-based national organizations—Presbyterians, Lutherans, Catholics—tap their respective local congregations. Catholic Charities USA also receives major funding from the dues of Catholic social welfare institutions and agencies under its wing (for example, Catholic Social Services of Green Bay, St. Ann's Home for the Aged in Rochester) and from diocesan payments.

The secular organizations use other means of fund-raising. World Hunger Year, an organization founded by the singer Harry Chapin, and Share Our Strength both rely heavily on benefit events, such as concerts and public readings by well-known authors. Share Our Strength also raises money through its annual Taste of the Nation, a month-long wine and food tasting event in 100 cities in which the entire proceeds are donated to various emergency food providers. In 1994 Taste of the Nation raised $3.7 million.

A number of anti-hunger organizations derive the bulk of their funding from corporate and foundation sources. Foodchain (whose benefactors are Phillip Morris, Coca-Cola, and the UPS Foundation), FRAC (Kraft General Foods, Gerber Foods, Ford Foundation), and the Tufts Center (Kraft General Foods, Hasbro, Ford Foundation) are examples. Share Our Strength also received corporate monies in the early 1990s through its Charge Against Hunger, a partnership with the American Express Company, whereby they received two or three cents every time someone used an American Express charge card. Each of the first two month-long campaigns raised more than $5 million.

Only a handful of corporate foundations are interested in hunger issues and organizations, but those that do provide grants appear to have marked out distinctive niches.[20] One of the first major corporate donors was the American Can Company Foundation, which funded the early surveys of emergency food providers conducted by the U.S. Conference of Mayors. In the mid-1990s the major corporate foundation donors were Phillip Morris and Kraft General Foods. The latter is a division of Phillip Morris with its own independent giving program. Phillip Morris has focused on programs aimed at needy adults, funding both providers and particular studies. Kraft General Foods funds programs aimed at children and has been a critical underwriter of FRAC and its Community Childhood Hunger Identification Project (CCHIP) survey and the Tufts Center for its work on the impact of undernutrition on children.

Not only do the anti-hunger groups tend to mine different funding veins, but they also have established an explicit division of labor. As the head of RESULTS commented, "Bob Greenstein [at the Center on Budget and Policy Priorities] is a genius at producing numbers; we're geniuses at waking people up."[21] And Larry Brown of Tufts notes that "FRAC is the leader in legislative advocacy. . . . Tufts is the intellectual heart of the movement. . . . Bill Shore [of Share Our Strength] is a genius at support for the network."[22] These kinds of comments illustrate four distinct missions that groups in the anti-hunger movement pursue: public education and mobilization; network support and management; research and resource functions; and lobbying and advocacy.

Education and mobilization encompass a wide range of activities: the Lutheran Office for Governmental Affairs issues periodic "Action Alert" bulletins to inform its congregations of pending decisions in food assistance policy and to urge people to write to their congressional representatives; World Hunger Year publishes a quarterly magazine, *Challenging Hunger and Poverty*; Bread for the World and RESULTS motivate people at the grassroots level to take action against hunger. World Hunger Year and RESULTS both take on the task of "telling the story of hunger to the media," the former by linking model anti-hunger groups and reporters, the latter by setting up conference call briefings of editorial writers and hunger advocates.[23] The Tufts Center distributes distillations of academic findings about the effects of undernutrition on children to policymakers and state hunger organizations.

Network support and management involves fund-raising for agencies and programs that deliver food to the needy, identifying and recognizing model or innovative programs, and setting operating standards for member organizations. Second Harvest, for example, certifies food banks that meet certain criteria. The Tufts Center provides leadership for the state hunger groups. World Hunger Year serves as a clearinghouse of information on model programs, while Share Our Strength is a major fund-raiser for anti-hunger groups at all levels. Catholic Charities USA serves its network of Catholic social agencies by providing technical assistance, training, and networking.

The research function is dominated by the Center on Budget and Policy Priorities and the Tufts Center and, to a lesser extent, FRAC. These organizations generate studies, gather raw data, synthesize existing research, and conduct program analyses. All are used for the purposes of political advocacy by the lobby organizations in the anti-hunger community. These studies provide material for congressional testimony, and they are used to educate the media.[24] Particular initiatives by the Center on Budget and Policy Priorities include dissemination of research on the effectiveness of WIC and on ways in which states can expand their outreach efforts to increase program participation.[25]

FRAC's major research contribution to the hunger movement has been CCHIP, the survey of childhood hunger undertaken in 1991. Both FRAC and the Tufts Center also perform secondary analyses of nutrition and hunger data and compile and circulate state-of-knowledge research on these topics. Thus FRAC released *Feeding the Other Half* in 1989, a report on the consequences of inadequate nutrition among those eligible for but not participating in WIC. The Tufts Center reports that it distributed more than 272,000 copies of eight reports in the first half of 1995.[26] The distribution list includes all members of Congress, the White House, state legislators and governors, the press, state hunger leaders, and various organizations. Among the most widely distributed reports were two that were part of the center's Nutrition-Cognition Initiative, exploring the relationship between nutrition and childhood development.[27]

Other groups contribute to the research enterprise as well: Second Harvest has done two major national surveys of food banks and their clientele; and Bread for the World, through its research and publishing wing, the Bread for the World Institute, produces an annual volume on the state of hunger in the world.

Finally there are the lobby organizations. Their representatives appear regularly at congressional hearings, they produce briefing papers for political officials, they hold news conferences and issue press releases to publicize their positions, and they walk the halls of Congress. At Representative Tony Hall's request, Bread for the World leader David Beckmann moderated a press conference on Capitol Hill to speak out against the 1995 Personal Responsibility Act, one of whose provisions, the denial of food assistance to legal immigrants, eventually became law under the 1996 welfare reform. The Tufts Center speaks publicly for the organizational and individual signers of the Medford Declaration, the commitment to work to end hunger in the United States. And Robert Fersh, head of FRAC, describes his organization as "a policy operation, working at all levels of government to get policy changed and to implement food assistance laws."[28]

Table 7-1 depicts each of the four missions as distinct domains that nevertheless overlap with each of the others. As the table shows, the various hunger organizations inhabit distinctive niches, or to put it another way, pursue distinctive missions or combinations of missions. Even though three organizations—the Tufts Center, Bread for the World, and FRAC—cluster in a multifunctional space at the center of the network, the other groups are arrayed in a relatively scattered fashion. The result is a clear set of organizational niches reflecting a division of labor among the major national anti-hunger groups. There is little opportunity for turf battles and few occasions where there is a risk of working at cross-purposes.

Coordinating the Hunger Network

A functional division of labor may facilitate a broad-front assault on the problem of hunger, but it does little to focus and aggregate the political power of the anti-hunger movement. A few organizations are capable of mobilizing their own grassroots constituencies to bring pressure on Congress, and several of these groups have the capacity to make considerable noise. Bread for the World claims that it can generate as many as a quarter million letters by working through its affiliate churches. The Lutheran advocacy office has a much smaller grassroots base, but it too works through congregations to send messages to Congress. RESULTS has a small network of secular grassroots organizations that it can ask to make calls or write letters, especially to the news media. It is particularly adept at persuading editorial writers to address hunger issues. But all these individual initiatives are episodic, and they often lack spontaneity.

More sustained efforts to bring political pressure to bear require informed advocacy by people who speak for the anti-hunger network and coordination among the various groups to demonstrate common purpose and unity. Such joint efforts have come about through both informal and formal means. In the informal realm there is a continual exchange of assistance and expertise at the leadership level among the groups, the purpose of which is to ensure that the various organizations in the anti-hunger network are working for the same ends with the same information. Thus FRAC people serve as a resource for the Food Policy Working Group, a coalition of religious organizations based in Washington. Sam Harris of RESULTS regularly briefs FRAC, Catholic Charities USA, the Children's Defense Fund, and other organizations about policy options and model

Table 7-1. *Functional Division of Labor among Anti-Hunger Groups*

Group	Type of activity			
	Education and grassroots mobilization	Network support and management	Research and resource development	Lobbying
Bread for the World	✓	✓	✓	✓
Food Research and Action Center	✓	✓	✓	✓
Tufts Center on Hunger, Poverty and Nutrition Policy	✓	✓	✓	✓
Second Harvest		✓	✓	✓
RESULTS	✓	✓		
World Hunger Year	✓		✓	✓
Center on Budget and Policy Priorities			✓	✓
Lutheran Office of Government Affairs	✓	✓		
Catholic Charities USA		✓		
Foodchain		✓		
Share Our Strength				

programs. David Beckmann has reached out to Catholic Charities USA and Second Harvest to advise those organizations on taking a more active political role in the anti-hunger movement.

Many of the exchanges of information and advice among the leaders of the major hunger groups occur in the context of explicit coalition-building efforts. According to Robert Fersh, "When there's a food bill up before Congress, we call all the groups together and strategize. . . . FRAC always has the hard information on how the food programs work, so groups come to us."[29] On several occasions FRAC has convened the leadership of the major national anti-hunger organizations even in the absence of pending legislation, simply to discuss common objectives and strategies.

Many of the religious organizations also meet together as the Food Policy Working Group, a coalition originally established to press Congress to pass the Mickey Leland Childhood Hunger Relief Act in 1993. The coalition survived beyond that successful campaign, continuing to lobby to preserve existing food assistance programs and to assure their full funding. The faith-based hunger groups were particularly active through this coalition in the effort in 1995 to stop the block granting of the food programs.

The most important source of coordination for political advocacy is the Tufts Center. The formal functions of the center, established in 1990, have been to document the extent of hunger in the United States, conduct and disseminate analyses of the effects of hunger, provide technical assistance to local and state anti-hunger organizations, and serve as a resource for corporations, the media, and members of Congress interested in the hunger issue.

Its major accomplishment, however, has been to give substance and direction to the anti-hunger network through the drafting and subsequent exploitation of the Medford Declaration. The declaration, a statement of commitment to end hunger in the United States, was conceived as a domestic equivalent of the Bellagio Declaration of 1989, which laid out a strategy for nations to conquer world hunger by the year 2000.[30] Once the declaration was drafted in Medford (Tufts' home in Massachusetts) by a committee made up of leaders from World Hunger Year, FRAC, and the Tufts Center, the drafters circulated the document among anti-hunger groups, corporations, celebrities, and politicians for their signatures. The purpose of the declaration was to enable anti-hunger interests "to focus on hunger from their own perspectives while being part of a common national agenda."[31] All the major national and many regional anti-hunger groups signed on, as well as seventy-five mayors, nine governors, and 2,500 individual corporate leaders and entertainers.[32] The Medford Declaration put the larger anti-hunger movement on record in support of expansion (to "fully use existing federal food programs") of school lunches and breakfasts, WIC, food stamps, and elderly feeding programs sufficient to cover every hungry person in the United States by 1995. Hunger, the declaration said, is "un-American."

As a guide to policy, the declaration itself has had only modest impacts. After a flurry of initial press coverage when the declaration was drafted, it was rarely mentioned again during the debates over Republican program cuts in the 104th Congress or in the subsequent welfare reform debate in which Congress significantly restricted access to food stamps. As a coordinating device, however, the declaration is regarded as the glue that holds the domestic anti-hunger movement together. Larry Brown of the Tufts Center sees the Medford Declaration as "the beginning of the hunger movement working together."[33] David Beckmann, president of Bread for the World, commented that "in the Medford group there has emerged a strong consensus and collective leadership. . . . There's a shared agenda, even though we all have our own mandates and boards and histories."[34]

To manage this coordination and create this consensus, the Tufts Center organizes conference calls among the organizational signatories to the declaration. Weekly calls, involving as many as fifteen anti-hunger groups at a time, are devoted to briefings and strategy discussions. The agenda for one conference call shortly after the congressional elections of 1994, for example, included a discussion of strategies for "responding to the changed political climate and the Contract With America."[35] The calls are used to forge a common posture among the anti-hunger organizations. In a memo summarizing a conference call in the late spring of 1993, Larry Brown pointed out that the forthcoming Hunger Forum organized by USDA would provide an occasion for "national hunger organizations to speak with one voice." He went on to note that parties to the conference call were in agreement that "it could prove highly beneficial if we spoke to and had general agreement on several key themes" as each group made its presentation at the Hunger Forum.[36] Brown then went on to list those themes: the importance of WIC in the short term, the need to identify poverty and income inequality as the root causes of hunger, and a reiteration of the Medford Declaration goals.

After the 1994 elections, Tufts Center leadership initiated a second series of conference calls limited to a select number of Medford signatories, a group that had in fact been meeting sporadically in New York and Washington. The large conference calls had become sessions devoted to the politics of the moment on Capitol Hill. There was no opportunity "to step back and think about ways of changing the public policy framework, of articulating a vision that would capture the public imagination. The big conference calls keep us focused on the trees, not the forest."[37] Thus the half dozen or so major anti-hunger groups—FRAC, the Tufts Center, Share Our Strength, World Hunger Year, Second Harvest, Bread for the World—constituted themselves in essence as the executive committee of the network.

This group drafted what it called an Omnibus Domestic Hunger bill, a proposal to expand all federal food programs, which became a focal point of the Tufts Center's strategy to mobilize and coordinate state anti-hunger groups. Shortly after the 1994 congressional elections, Brown wrote to state hunger leaders urging them to fight Republican efforts to cut food assistance programs. "The Center," he wrote, "is creating several products that we hope are useful to you as you work with your Congressional delegations and state legislatures to avert regressive measures at both the national and state levels." One of those "products" was the Omnibus Domestic Hunger Bill, which state organizations could use as a policy counterpoint to the proposed cuts.[38]

Speaking with One Voice

It would hardly be surprising if organizations divided by religious issues, organizational design, resource disparities, and a range of strategic preferences simply pursued their own paths in the effort to eradicate hunger. The absence of the hunger select committee as an institutional focal point reinforces the expectation that the hunger community of voluntary groups could easily fly apart as a result of sheer centrifugal force. But in fact, by the mid-1990s an executive committee of the anti-hunger movement had arisen by a process of natural selection. The leadership was able to convene the hunger organizations on a regular basis, propose or work out common positions, and speak on Capitol Hill for the movement. The decisions of this leadership group not only determined strategy in the politics of domestic hunger but, with the congressional anti-hunger forces without an institutional base, also played the major role in setting the hunger policy agenda.

If the executive committee articulates the position of the collective hunger movement, what factors account for the willingness of the various groups to assent to this leadership? Why does this diverse anti-hunger community manage to speak with one voice? In part the chances of unity might be expected to increase in a situation in which established programs are under threat, as the federal food assistance programs were in the 104th Congress. Although the anti-hunger groups disagree to some extent about whether the programs are an end in themselves, and they differ too on whether to put the bulk of their own resources into the fight against hunger at home or hunger abroad, there is solid support not only for maintaining federal food assistance but expanding it. Commitment to domestic public food assistance is an important common denominator.

Yet the anti-hunger movement did not always take a purely defensive posture; the Medford Declaration and the Omnibus Domestic Hunger Bill, offensive initiatives, were both promoted in the mid-1990s, despite the strong political forces pushing for funding reductions and block granting of food assistance programs. Thus the cohesiveness of the anti-hunger movement is not merely a product of its defense of the core programs.

Perhaps a more important source of the cohesiveness of the anti-hunger community lies in what Émile Durkheim described a century ago as the interdependence that derives from the division of labor among groups engaged in even the most general common enterprise. "Great political societies," he wrote, "can maintain themselves in equilibrium only thanks to the specialization of tasks [wherein] the division of labor is the source, if not unique, at least principal, of social solidarity."[39] Embracing the common purpose—the eradication of hunger in this case—is a first condition of cohesion, but it is not sufficient in itself. What produces cohesion is that each group needs the others to perform different roles in the campaign: fund-raising, grassroots mobilization, research and analysis, and lobbying. A leadership cadre is important not only to articulate the common views but also to call into play the various roles that organizations play within the hunger community. The organizations in the hunger movement then have transformed their differences into a strength through a combination of astute leadership and a functional division of labor.

8 | *Charitable Food Assistance: The Volunteer Sector*

Although most food assistance to the needy in the United States is paid for by the federal government, private nonprofit charitable organizations are important participants in both delivering and supplementing those efforts. By playing a role in the delivery process, nonprofit organizations serve to leverage the resources provided by public programs, thus extending the reach of government. Through their own charitable efforts, the nonprofits also feed clients who cannot or do not wish to receive direct assistance from the government or who cannot fill their needs within the constraints of public programs.

Yet if government relies on charitable organizations to implement public programs and extend its reach, so too does the nonprofit sector depend on government. Private food assistance organizations receive on average far more money from the various levels of government than from corporate, individual, and foundation sources combined.[1] Many charitable organizations involved in feeding receive foodstuffs from public stocks as well. For example, in her ethnography of a Connecticut church-based soup kitchen, Irene Glasser describes the office of the manager as "piled high with surplus food from the USDA," and an official with Second Harvest estimates that on average about 13.4 percent of food distributed through programs in its network, both secular and religious, comes from the federal government.[2] Thus public and private sectors in hunger assistance are deeply entwined, so much so that one cannot understand the American food assistance system without understanding its partnership elements.

In this respect the delivery of food assistance is part of a broader pattern in the provision of social services in the United States in which both public and private sectors bring their respective strengths to bear on the task at hand and supplement one another's efforts. Whereas the virtues of government lie in its relatively vast resources and its legitimacy in setting priorities in a democratic society, the nonprofit sector, as Lester Salamon and his colleagues have pointed out, has long been valued in the service delivery process for its smaller and more humane scale, its often greater flexibility vis-à-vis government, its access to volunteer labor, and its ability to tap charitable impulses among the public.[3]

Delivering food to the needy through this partnership arrangement is not without its problems, however. For example, some of the nonprofit sector's virtues—flexibility and scale—are offset by problems characteristic of many voluntary organizations, such as underfunding and lack of professionalism. The results of these may include an inability or unwillingness to offer universal coverage, inconstant and sometimes unreliable service, simple ineptitude, and even occasional corruption. In addition, the food assistance provided by many (though not all) nonprofit organizations may be designed to further or at least accompany a larger, and perhaps only tangentially related, agenda. Whereas government provides food as part of both its welfare obligation and its desire to invest in the future human capital stock, religious organizations may see food aid as a way to spread their message among the recipients of help as well as in their own congregations. Nonprofits, too, may use hunger relief to serve other purposes: some, such as RESULTS, provide food assistance as part of a broader effort to organize the dispossessed.

In a more general light, the use of private, voluntary organizations as such integral components in the food assistance system is a product of American skepticism about public welfare. Private charity is viewed by many as preferable to government assistance: it seems to be less rule-bound and less formally institutionalized; it is given willingly; it offers the opportunity for ordinary individuals to take helping actions, thus providing a measure of personal satisfaction and moral relief. But one problem with the vision of neighbors helping neighbors is that the more numerous the nonprofit channels are for individuals to satisfy their moral impulses, the less political support there is for expanded public welfare. If nonprofit food assistance could substitute for government food assistance in quantity, quality, and coverage, this might not be a problem. But private efforts are manifestly inadequate to the size of the task of feeding the hungry and the food-insecure. Thus, ironically, the elaboration of private charitable food assistance may in the end actually impede the conquest of hunger.

Organizations

Charitable efforts to feed the hungry enjoy a visible presence in the nation and in the larger nonprofit community. Share Our Strength, for example, gained wide national publicity in the print and television media through its link to major corporate partners such as American Express and Northwest Airlines. Among charitable organizations of all types, Second Harvest has ranked as high as third in the nation in the value of its annual private donations, mostly in the form of food, behind only the United Jewish Appeal and the Salvation Army. In the early 1990s Second Harvest ranked ahead of such major organizations as the Red Cross, Catholic Charities USA, the American Cancer Society, and the YMCA.[4]

But in general, despite the visibility of some of its individual organizational members, the community of hunger assistance groups is not particularly well endowed, as we observed in chapter 7. Of all types of social service organizations with tax-exempt status that are not affiliated with churches or synagogues, the nearly 1,200 organizations devoted to free food distribution that filed with the Internal Revenue Service for 501(C)(3) designation tend to rank collectively at or just below the median in terms of total assets, average size of gift, and total gifts, grants, and contributions.[5] The average assets of individual hunger assistance organizations are among the lowest of all organizations in the charitable social service sector. Individual hunger assistance groups are less well endowed on average than the average individual organizations devoted to legal services, child services, crime prevention, emergency services, aid to the homeless, substance abuse, or crisis intervention.[6]

Voluntary feeding organizations are also small in relation to government efforts. David Beckmann estimates that private feeding groups are responsible for giving away about $4 billion worth of food per year.[7] Not all of this is purchased with private donations. Some comes from the nearly $40 billion the federal government spends annually on food assistance: Washington gives the nonprofits cash to spend on food purchases as well as commodities to be distributed. Second Harvest reports that purely private food donations amount to no more than $2 billion to $2.5 billion per year.[8]

In chapter 7 we examined the major national hunger assistance organizations, many of which serve an umbrella function for street-level operations. Unfortunately, there is no reliable census of these latter organizations, which include soup kitchens, food pantries, and various sorts of congregate feeding facilities attached to institutions such as shelters and day care centers. Food pantries are certainly the workhorses of the voluntary street-level institutions dedicated principally to feeding. Their total number remains elusive, however. In the 1993 study of Second Harvest operations and clients, researchers estimated that the national organization served as an umbrella for 69,294 food programs, of which about 27,000 (38.9 percent) were food pantries. Soup kitchens, the other type of dedicated feeding organization, numbered about 4,100 (7 percent). Multipurpose organizations that offer free food as well as other services accounted for the remainder, including about 5,500 emergency shelters for the homeless, battered women, runaway teens, and so on (8.9 percent of the programs in the Second Harvest network), and about 33,000 group homes, day care facilities, senior citizen centers, and summer camps (accounting for 47 percent).

Second Harvest organizations account for only a portion of all street-level feeding operations, however. For example, the Bread for the World Institute has estimated on the basis of its own survey data that about 150,000 food pantries were affiliated with religious congregations in the United States in the early 1990s.[9]

Even if there are no precise figures, however, it is clear that the number of street-level feeding organizations has grown rapidly. The 1993 Second Harvest survey estimates that 71 percent of its local programs were established after 1981; almost half (46.5 percent) were set up after 1986.[10] Such feeding operations are now standard features in the food assistance systems of both urban and rural communities in most parts of the country.

Volunteers

Nearly everyone in the United States claims to have helped the hungry at one time or another. A nationwide poll conducted in 1992 among 1,000 registered voters found that 79 percent answered affirmatively to the question, "Have you, personally, done anything to help those people who don't have enough to eat in your community, such as being a volunteer at a soup kitchen, contributing food to a distribution center, and so forth?"[11]

Although these numbers may seem high, they are not implausible: bringing a can of food to the pantry in one's church or synagogue or giving a donation at the door in response to a scout or school food drive are close to universal experiences among middle- and working-class Americans.

More sustained volunteer help in providing food to the needy—cooking or serving food at a soup kitchen, driving a truck to collect surplus food from grocery stores, stacking donations in warehouses—is far less common, although we know very little of its actual dimensions. In general, Americans engage heavily in volunteer work, but surveys indicate that most of this activity is done for religious, health, or educational organizations or in an informal way.[12] These surveys do not compile data specifically on volunteer efforts to gather and deliver food to the needy, although this is an activity that the Independent Sector classifies under the broad category of "social services and welfare." That entire category claims less than 10 percent of all volunteer assignments.

The 1993 Second Harvest study provides more specific data on volunteering in food assistance organizations, although its figures are limited to organizations in the Second Harvest network. Food pantries in the network reported an average of 2.1 paid employees but slightly more than thirty-eight volunteer workers over the course of the prior year.[13] Soup kitchens, labor-intensive operations, attract a larger supply of volunteers. Although they also employed on average slightly more than two people, the typical kitchen was able to count on 166 volunteers. Shelters and group institutions involved in feeding had slightly higher numbers of paid workers (6.1 and 7, respectively). The former organizations could count on about ninety-seven volunteers per year; the latter on just over fifty-eight. Extrapolating to its entire network of more than 69,000 different sorts of feeding organizations, Second Harvest estimates that at least 831,528 people volunteered their services in the year prior to the survey to provide food in an organizational setting to the needy.

The Virtues of Private Charity

The voluntary anti-hunger organizations are essential components of the American food assistance system. They are important vehicles for mobilizing public concern, and they serve to tap private charitable impulses, generating in-kind food donations, monetary contributions, and volunteer labor. Not the least of their virtues is their unique access to raw, processed, and prepared foods that would otherwise go to waste. No government food program intentionally taps this huge resource of food originally intended for the retail or hospitality markets and distributes it to the needy. Second Harvest food banks, Foodchain member agencies, New York's CityHarvest, and other gleaning operations are important vehicles for reducing such waste. But beyond these important functions, the volunteer sector makes other key contributions to the effort to feed hungry people.

Leveraging Government Resources

Certain federal food assistance programs, including food stamps, are administered entirely by government entities, but charitable organizations and volunteers are key partners in the implementation of others. Several programs would either not be implemented at all without volunteers or would be far smaller in scope. Michael Lipsky's study of TEFAP, for example, argues that volunteer labor has been crucial to the distribution of federal surplus commodities.[14] Richard Hoehn estimates that 350,000 people volunteer daily at elderly congregate feeding sites or deliver Meals on Wheels, while a study of the summer food service found a heavy reliance on volunteer student, teacher, and parent labor.[15]

Lester Salamon and his colleagues have called this sort of partnership "nonprofit federalism," whereby government is able to provide or extend services without expanding the formal bureaucracy or public work force.[16] The attractiveness of such a partnership for government is particularly evident when the value of volunteer labor is taken into consideration.[17] We get some inkling of the dimensions of the contribution from Second Harvest's estimate that the total value of volunteer labor in all of its programs runs at about $434 million per year.[18] Some undetermined fraction of that is involved in distributing TEFAP and other commodities through Second Harvest programs.

Expanding Food Assistance

Charitable food groups function not only to deliver but also to supplement and even to substitute for government aid. All of these roles are increasingly common in the provision of social services in the United States.[19] The charitable effort to serve people for whom government assistance is inadequate or who do not or cannot seek public food aid is perhaps the most important contribution of the voluntary sector in the food assistance system.

Empirical studies show clearly that some of the clients of charitable food programs do not participate in any sort of public food assistance. Beth Daponte's investigation of Pittsburgh food pantry users found that 9.4 percent of her low-income sample—disproportionately elderly people—relied only on private food pantries rather than food stamps for assistance, even though they were eligible for the latter.[20] Another study found that even among a sample of single, low-income women with young children in Michigan, few used food pantries rather than food stamps.[21]

The most dramatic data demonstrating the niche role of private food charity is provided by the Second Harvest survey of its clients. Less than half (47.5 percent) of the nearly 26 million clients of feeding programs in the network receive food stamps. Among those Second Harvest clients who do not receive food stamps, only 30.1 percent say they are not eligible. Of the remainder, nearly as many (27.8 percent) say they do not want to apply, and another 10.3 percent say it is not worth the trouble. Slightly more than 10 percent of the users of charitable food services either do not know about the food stamp program or do not know how to apply.[22]

Among elderly clients of Second Harvest programs, only 25 percent visited federally funded senior lunch sites, and only 9 percent used the Meals on Wheels program. Surprisingly small numbers of people with small children who rely on food pantries and soup kitchens also avail themselves of WIC (31 percent), school lunch or breakfast (57 percent), child care food (7 percent), or summer food service (13 percent).[23]

The voluntary sector also plays a role in supplementing federal food programs. Of those who do receive food stamps and yet also obtain food from charitable organizations, 82 percent say that the food stamps run out before the end of the month, making a visit to a network pantry or soup kitchen essential.

Informality and Flexibility

Clearly, a substantial demand exists for food assistance that government programs do not address. Some clients of charity food programs may not meet federal eligibility standards. Others may be too proud to participate in government programs. Mental illness or substance abuse may prevent other clients from taking the necessary steps to apply for formal assistance. The virtue of help provided by the voluntary sector is that it is generally proffered with no questions asked.[24] It represents, as Glasser makes clear in her study of the soup kitchen, a form of "hassle-free" help. Clients, or "guests" as they are called in the soup kitchen, have no caseworkers, no files, no application hurdles. The apparent informality and flexibility of the voluntary sector thus makes possible service to those shut out of what appears to them to be a rigid, bureaucratic, public social service system.[25]

Some voluntary charitable organizations impose no eligibility standards at all. Those that do—as they must if federal commodity distribution is involved—may follow quite informal or loose certification procedures. For example, in the forty-four food pantries in south central Wisconsin, some run by religious congregations, others not, volunteers must ask recipients of federal surpluses or TEFAP food to attest that their income is 150 percent or less than the official poverty line. No rigorous proof is required, however, which is a sharp contrast to detailed income and assets documentation that food stamp recipients must provide.[26]

Most of the food given out in these Wisconsin pantries comes from private sources. For this food, thirty-two of the forty-four pantries impose no eligibility requirements on recipients at all. The remainder limit their services to people who reside in a particular geographic area (for example, a certain school district), but require no proof of need. Half the pantries do not even require a referral. Many of those that do ask for a referral by a church or social service agency nevertheless make clear that they will not turn anyone away.[27]

Daponte's study of Pittsburgh food pantries found a different pattern: 60 percent set an income threshold, though none asks about assets. Of the remaining pantries, however, 30 percent require only residence in a particular geographic area or membership in the sponsoring church. Ten percent, like most of their Wisconsin counterparts, impose no eligibility standards at all.[28]

The Volunteer Service Ethic

The charitable social service sector is prized for the supposed commitment and compassion of its volunteers. Volunteers, who act from caring rather than pecuniary or professional motives, humanize assistance. In Lipsky's words, volunteer workers in food pantries are "neighbors, rich and poor, [who] assist other neighbors in need."[29] One notion that underlies these suppositions is that formal bureaucracies reduce worker autonomy and impose routinization, thus dulling the commitment of employees, eroding their interest in the job, and compromising performance.

Though the generalization both about the nature of bureaucracies and the effects on workers may be debatable, some very modest though suggestive evidence exists in particular in the charitable food assistance sector. Cruz Torres, Mary Zey, and William McIntosh have studied the effects of different degrees of bureaucratization (measured here by variations in opportunities for participation by volunteer staff in decisionmaking) on volunteer commitment among a number of food pantries in south Texas. Commitment is measured by willingness to give time and transportation resources to the organization. They found that the less bureaucratic pantries tend to have more committed volunteer workers. Such commitment, in the view of the authors, translates into organizational effectiveness, that is, the sense that the organization is serving client needs. In short, volunteers who work in organizations characterized by democratic decisionmaking rather than centralized executive control are better at serving the needy. The contrast with bureaucrats who staff public social service agencies, typically organized as formal hierarchies, is implicit.[30]

The Costs of Privatizing Food Assistance

Few would deny the importance of the role of the charitable voluntary sector in providing food to the needy. Compared with the public sector, however, private food charity is a relatively small component of the overall anti-hunger effort. In addition, certain problems inherent in the charitable provision of welfare strongly militate against extensive privatization.

The Insufficiency of Private Food Assistance

Hunger activists have long recognized that private feeding efforts are insufficient to solve the problem of hunger and food insecurity. Nor do they have the capacity to expand their efforts significantly. Even the largest and most successful charitable feeding organizations maintain no illusions about their ability to meet the demand for assistance. As the federal budget for social services was being cut in the early 1990s, leaders of the volunteer food sector publicly doubted their ability to make up for the losses.[31]

In an effort to anticipate the implications for the charitable sector of cuts in the food stamp program promulgated by the 1996 welfare reform bill, Second Harvest asked the Tufts Center to conduct an analysis of whether the agencies in its network could possibly make up the shortfall.[32] The Personal Responsibility and Work Opportunity Reconciliation Act of 1996 projects cuts of $28 billion from the food stamp program between 1997 and 2002, enough to buy approximately 24 billion pounds of food for the needy. This poses a formidable deficit for charitable feeding organizations to make up. In 1992 Second Harvest agencies were already reporting that they needed an additional 121 million pounds of food per year—17 percent of what they were distributing—in order to meet demand. It was estimated that to close this gap (which the analysts held constant) as well as make up the additional deficit caused by the food stamp cuts, Second Harvest agencies would have to increase their food acquisition by 425 percent over their 1995 capacity by 2002. Since the annual rate of growth in food acquisition in fact was barely more than 5 percent between 1991 and 1995, filling the gap was clearly regarded as far out of reach.

Second Harvest agencies comprise the largest and one of the most solidly established of the voluntary food charities. Other organizations, particularly those less well connected to national umbrella institutions, suffer chronic shortfalls as well. It is common for food pantries to ration their assistance. Even in relatively flush times, most outlets supply little more than a few days' worth of food at infrequent intervals. In the survey of south central Wisconsin food pantries, for example, only eight of the forty-four allowed people to get groceries more often than once a month; twenty-eight permitted visits only once a month; and eight restricted visits to once every sixty days or more.

Food assistance provided by charitable organizations, therefore, is fundamentally inadequate as a sole source of food for the needy. As a report by the House Select Committee on Hunger acknowledged, "Emergency methods, such as food pantries and soup kitchens, provide only limited and temporary solutions to a long-term complex problem."[33]

Lack of Dependability

Charitable resources, both donations and volunteer labor, tend to fluctuate with the season. Most activity occurs between Thanksgiving and the new year. At other times, many pantries and soup kitchens struggle to keep open. One of the most serious problems is that volunteer commitment tends to flag, producing high turnover rates. Janet Poppendieck writes that "burnout is rampant among volunteers and program directors." In some communities there is a steady flow of new recruits, but "recruiting and training volunteers . . . requires considerable investment, and many volunteers prove to be short term."[34]

Many volunteers in fact are not trained in any way. An official involved in the commodity distribution program of the 1960s complained before Congress that the volunteers who predominated in the program "were neither skilled nor trained in interviewing and verifying resources."[35] Volunteers are, by definition, not professionals, and their lack of professionalism was a chronic problem in the federal commodity distribution program. In the 1980s states responded to USDA mandates by requiring the local volunteer organizations involved in distributing TEFAP commodities to determine the eligibility of clients and to keep records of their names and the amounts of food they received. Many volunteers felt that these "bureaucratic" requirements were so burdensome that they ceased to donate their time. Volunteers were also reluctant to ask people for proof of eligibility. In New Jersey the Salvation Army dropped out of the program altogether for lack of volunteers.[36]

It is true that funding for public programs may also rise and fall as the political winds shift, but public programs are difficult to terminate altogether. In any event, the fortunes of public social programs are the product of a collective debate, a social decision process, not the vagaries of the countless individual predilections to give or not to give that determine the fortunes of private charities. This means that changes in public programs may acquire a certain legitimacy, or at least a degree of political logic. In addition, public programs are staffed by professionals, providing consistency and continuity in program administration.

Religious Agendas

Most major religions teach their adherents to care for the needy.[37] In the United States most Jewish and Christian groups maintain national organizations devoted to welfare work, including food assistance, and some, such as Mazon or the Presbyterian Hunger Program, are dedicated exclusively to hunger relief. At the street level, most feeding operations are affiliated with religious congregations. In the huge Second Harvest network, for example, 71.1 percent of the pantries and 70.8 percent of the soup kitchens are sponsored by churches.[38] In Connecticut 80 percent of the soup kitchens are run by Christian churches.[39] In the survey of south central Wisconsin pantries, eighteen of the forty-four were church-affiliated, and three others were run by the Salvation Army or the YWCA.

It is not known precisely how many of these pantries or soup kitchens proselytize their clients, nor is there evidence that clients object when it does occur. Many congregation-based programs have policies of serving anyone who seeks help, and federal law prohibits street-level agencies involved in TEFAP or federal commodity distribution from engaging clients in any religious activity. Glasser did not observe overt proselytizing in the soup kitchen she studied, although the facility was run by a church as part of its ministry to the poor.

Nevertheless, some religious activity does go on. In the Connecticut soup kitchen volunteers made it clear that they saw their participation as an opportunity to put their religious faith to work, and each meal began with a brief Christian prayer, usually offered by the director of the facility.[40] In one Wisconsin city, the pastor at a congregate feeding site that used federal commodities refused to give up the mealtime prayer, and the local Community Action Commission withdrew the commodities.[41] In some counties in Wisconsin, church-based food banks include religious pamphlets in the bags of groceries.[42] In Texas Second Harvest arranged with a number of church-affiliated food banks to distribute federal commodities, but became uneasy when reports came in that proselytizing was occurring.[43]

Some organizations are clear about proffering a religious message with their charity. The Salvation Army runs one of the largest networks of feeding centers in the country. In 1992 it served more than 65 million meals in 8,000 centers with the help of 1.3 million volunteers.[44] According to Glasser, the Salvation Army seeks to provide "spiritual-religious therapy": people can get "shelter, meals, and alcohol rehabilitation if they go to the frequent church services that sometimes include testimonies of their belief in Christ."[45]

Whether religious proselytizing is common among street-level food providers or not, some clearly does occur. Moreover, even where no overt effort is made to communicate a religious principle, there is an implicit tension between society's desire to provide for anyone in need and the religious motivations and resources that make such assistance possible. For example, the provision of welfare to needy members of the public as part of a religious ministry raises issues of whose interests are central. Feeding the poor may be as useful to organized religion as it is to the food insecure and hungry to the extent that such activities mobilize and channel religious belief among volunteers and provide an occasion for teaching them a religious message. Any system of welfare assistance that relies heavily on religious institutions to supplement state assistance or to implement public programs thus risks a high level of civil and religious entanglement.

Lack of Regulation

With the exception of food stamps and commodity distribution, federal food assistance programs seek to provide nutritionally balanced assistance. Clients of food pantries and soup kitchens, however, receive whatever food these agencies collect through donations or purchase. Since bags of groceries and prepared meals are constituted according to what is in stock rather than according to nutrition guidelines, a diet based on these food sources may or may not be balanced. Glasser observed, for example, that fresh fruits and vegetables were rarely available at the soup kitchen she studied. No government regulations guide the composition of grocery bags or the content of meals, planning for which is left in the hands of individual program directors. Frequently, no professional nutritionist or dietician is involved.[46]

Of potentially greater concern than haphazard nutrition is that clients of volunteer food programs have no legally enforceable rights.[47] Given fluctuations in food stocks in charitable pantries, clients cannot count on receiving a set amount of food on a regular basis. Nor is there a system of due process to protect client access to private food assistance.

Geographic Maldistribution

As Poppendieck points out, food pantries and soup kitchens are established "wherever someone is moved to start one. There is no mechanism for allocating such endeavors evenly among areas of need."[48] This produces occasionally dramatic geographic inequities. In New York state, for example, service capacity provided by charitable food programs ranges from an ability to help five people per week for every 1,000 below the poverty line to 100 people per week for every 1,000 below the poverty line. Cathy Campbell calls this a "fragmented and somewhat fragile statewide alternate food distribution system."[49]

Areas of low population density are poorly served and many of these are parts of the country with a high proportion of rural poor. A map of the location of the 180 or so Second Harvest food banks shows that none are located in the entire states of Montana, Wyoming, or Utah.[50] Northern Wisconsin and the Upper Peninsula of Michigan, places with chronic high unemployment, do not have Second Harvest food banks, nor do the Four Corners area in the Southwest, southern and central Oregon, or the western Dakotas.

These patterns suggest that private food assistance is dependent to some extent on the location and prosperity of donors. In areas of high poverty or unemployment, such as Indian reservations or the northern Midwest, few sources of private charity exist, at least compared with demand. Thus both the existence of charitable food programs and their stocks of food vary from region to region.

Private Charity, Public Welfare, and Personal Goals

Although private food charity plays an important role in the system of hunger relief in the United States, it must be understood as an imperfect resolution of several fundamental tensions. One of these involves the tension between the genuine desire to help the hungry and the resistance to creating or sufficiently endowing the public institutions to accomplish this task. The result of this resolution is that American society has two systems of hunger relief, and though they complement one another to some extent, neither in the end is perfectly adequate. As long as the charitable sector is perceived as an alternative to the system of public food assistance or even as a safety net for those not served by government aid, there will be little pressure to support or augment the public programs.

Another tension lies in the complex motives of both voluntary organizations and the individual volunteers, namely the clash between the impulse to help the less fortunate and the desire to serve one's own organizational, spiritual, or moral needs through charitable good works.[51] The embrace of charity for these mixed motives necessarily raises questions about the primacy of the interests of those who are helped and the degree to which those interests are perfectly understood by the givers. By definition, charity, even in its most altruistic form, is given according to the giver's terms: the amount, the form, the timing, and the conditions may or may not conform to the recipient's needs. In a charitable relationship, the recipient has few claims and no entitlements. As anthropologist Mary Douglas has observed, "Giving food away unilaterally makes an asymmetrical relation. The lopsided food gift loads the recipient's status with demeaning signs."[52]

That much charitable work springs in part from the desire to satisfy one's own needs is abundantly clear. Consider one of the more successful fund-raising devices run by Share Our Strength. Taste of the Nation enlists

Table 8-1. *Personal Motivations for Giving and Volunteering,*
All Charities, 1992

Motivation	Percent[a]
Moral imperative	
Feeling that those who have more should help those who have less	54.6
Meeting religious beliefs or commitments	41.0
Giving back to society some of the benefits it gave to you	39.1
Serving as an example for others	30.5
Self-satisfaction	
Gaining a sense of personal satisfaction	43.2
Instrumental reasons	
Ensuring continuation of activities or institutions from which I or my family benefit	34.1
Fulfilling a business or community obligation	19.3
Creating a remembrance of me or my family	17.0
Receiving tax deductions	12.0
Being encouraged by an employer	9.9

Source: Based on data from Independent Sector, *Giving and Volunteering in the United States* (Washington, D.C.: Independent Sector, 1992).

a. Respondents gave motive as a major reason for giving and volunteering. Because respondents provided more than one answer, totals do not add up to 100 percent.

the country's great chefs to donate food and an evening of their time to prepare meals to serve at a benefit whose proceeds go for hunger relief. There is an obvious irony in raising money for the hungry by serving elaborate meals, but what is less obvious is that it is far easier to get the participation of the chefs in this sort of event than it is to get them simply to write a check to Share Our Strength.[53] Cooking for the hunger benefit not only presumably helps the hungry, but putting one's skills to work for a good cause is also personally and professionally satisfying for the chefs.

A national survey conducted by the Gallup organization for Independent Sector in 1992 suggests that although many people apparently volunteer for the purest of altruistic motives (almost 55 percent of the respondents say that "the feeling that those who have more should help those with less" is a major reason for giving), many more do so to gain a sense of moral satisfaction or to fulfill some instrumental purpose, such as meeting some business or personal obligation (see table 8-1).[54]

What is finally important about a substantial reliance on charitable giving is that the mix of motives that underlies giving helps to shape the contours of private food assistance in distinctive ways that do not necessarily serve the interests of the needy. For example, these motives may lead people to give at holiday time when claims are made on their moral or religious sense rather than at other times. Such motives may lead people to give to organizations chosen not for their effectiveness but for who sits on the board of directors. And such motives may lead people to give in ways that serve more to enhance their own self-image than to augment the resources of the hunger relief effort. Seen in this light, the role of private, voluntary anti-hunger organizations in an ideal food assistance system can only be to serve as minor partners, filling in the cracks that occur in government programs.

9 | *Toward an End to Hunger*

Three important hunger-related developments occurred within a six-month period in 1997: a dozen members of the House of Representatives from both parties, supported by an additional ninety-nine cosponsors, introduced the Hunger Has a Cure Act; the new provisions of the Personal Responsibility and Work Opportunity Reconciliation Act of 1996 (PRWORA) cutting food stamp benefits and eligibility rolls went into effect; and USDA released its long-awaited first report on the prevalence of household food security in the United States.

Each of these developments is important for understanding the status of the hunger problem in the United States at the close of the century. The release of the report on household food security marks a cognitive watershed in the effort to deal with American hunger. The substance and the methodology of the report are products of a hard-won consensus among all relevant parties on the idea of food insecurity. Furthermore, the survey results themselves provide the first detailed national demographic portrait of the prevalence of various levels of food deprivation. There is still much to learn about food insecurity among Americans, but a firmer base than ever before has been established. It is no longer possible to argue that the United States has failed to solve its hunger problem because Americans do not know its nature or its scope.

Nevertheless, the anti-hunger forces in Congress seemed to be, as they have often been, operating from the margins of the legislative process. The Hunger Has a Cure Act had more than a hundred sponsors, but it was not a priority for the House leadership of either party or for the White House. The act called for increased or full funding of existing food assistance programs, a "cure" that assumes that the basic policy apparatus is in place to deal with the problem.[1]

Yet the bill's sponsors had not only to contend with their lack of a strong institutional and political base in Congress but also with the countervailing forces represented by PRWORA. This welfare reform legislation not only cut funding for child nutrition programs and food stamps, but it continued a long pattern of restrictive and even punitive implementation, including the imposition of severe new food stamp eligibility rules that eliminated nearly all legal immigrants and many able-bodied citizens without dependents.[2]

The welfare bill achieves budget savings by weakening what was already a very thin food safety net serving the most needy. For example, more than 10 percent of the total savings in the bill comes about by reducing food stamp benefits from 103 percent of the cost of the Thrifty Food Plan to 100 percent.[3] Such a reduction may appear small, but it cuts into what the Center on Budget and Policy Priorities has already characterized as "a rather spartan diet, with less meat, poultry, fish, cheese, and eggs, and more dry beans and grain products than most Americans eat."[4] Along with a freeze on the standard deduction, which determines a household's disposable income and thus its food stamp allocation, the reduction to 100 percent of the Thrifty Food Plan will cut the typical participant's monthly food spending power by about 10 percent by 2002.

Some of the cuts in the food stamp program are offset by a requirement in the welfare bill for a modest new appropriation of $600 million (through 2002) for emergency commodity distribution to the needy. But to substitute emergency commodity assistance for food stamps is to provide assistance that is not only less predictable and less easily tailored to individual household needs but also less nutritionally balanced than the typical food stamp grocery basket.

Welfare reform effects other changes that suggest a characteristic disjunction between policy design and implementation. The thrust of policy design in the food stamp program has generally been toward greater national standardization. Although some states were permitted, beginning in the 1980s, to experiment with cash benefits and electronic benefit transfer cards rather than food stamps, eligibility standards and guarantees were nationalized in response to the inequities produced in the early years by states' ability to opt out of the program or, once in, to establish income and asset limits.[5] The 1996 law, however, significantly increases state discretion and control over program rules, calculation of households' shelter deductions, and other administrative aspects. Although some state flexibility may soften new federal constraints (for example, governors may seek waivers of the rule removing able-bodied adults from the food stamp rolls in high unemployment areas), the potential for interstate differences in food stamp implementation is greatly increased.

Policy Learning: What We Know

The policy community now knows a great deal about the nature of hunger in America. Hunger is not the same as malnutrition, nor is it typically the life-threatening condition that afflicts people in the third world. Lack of access to an abundant food supply rather than scarcity is the essence of the American hunger problem. We understand that lack of access is often a function of poverty, even though most poor people are not hungry. Among the deprived, we know that there are degrees of need. We have come to distinguish between people who cannot count confidently on obtaining adequate, regular food—the food insecure—and those who suffer the real physical distress that we call hunger. We have finally begun to measure the scope of these various conditions and their demographic correlates.

We know that the public food assistance programs, though inadequate for some and never generous, do work for many poor and near-poor, filling the gap between their ability to acquire food with their own resources and an adequate diet. Hunger programs themselves are no longer experimental. The pilot programs of the 1960s and 1970s, modified time and again, have long since become permanent. Furthermore, the payoffs are clear. Feeding children lunch in school increases nutritional intake; for every dollar's worth of milk and eggs provided lactating poor mothers $3.50 is saved in future medical costs; and good childhood nutrition aids cognitive development.

Yet public food aid does not save all people from deprivation. The reason can be traced less to a lack of knowledge about how to solve the problem than to the quality of our concern. Americans harbor unshakable doubts about the scope and severity of hunger, and the result is a failure of political will. It is not that Americans have done nothing; it is simply that they have not done enough. Thus we have designed an arsenal of programs because hunger in a rich land is deeply troubling, but at the same time many believe that those who get free food are freeloaders, that people who do not work ought not rely on those who do to pay for their food, that failing to get enough to eat in a food-rich society is the fault of the hungry, that many immigrants have come to the United States to feed in the welfare trough, and that the best help is given in the form of charity by volunteers. So food assistance policy is grudging: we erect administrative hurdles to participation in public programs, we eschew outreach, we bar whole categories of people from the eligibility rolls to suit the political temper of the times, and we limit funding in a way that almost guarantees insufficiency.

What We Do Right

Nevertheless, the basic structure of an effective and compassionate public food assistance effort is in place: a universal means-tested program, combined with targeted programs to serve the especially vulnerable. The food stamp program earmarks assistance for food but provides flexibility to accommodate household eating preferences and cooking capacities. The creation of smaller targeted programs is based on the recognition that children and the elderly, especially, often cannot acquire and prepare food for themselves and may have special dietary needs. It may be that they cannot count on family members or guardians to feed them regularly or it may be that they are children who need supplemental or high nutrient feeding in their formative years that even well-managed poor households cannot provide. Thus the food assistance system diversifies the sources and institutions involved in feeding vulnerable groups (school, summer camp, day care, elderly congregate meal sites), and designs that assistance to cover the life course and the rhythms of the year. In 1995 Congress resisted consolidating the separate child nutrition programs and turning them over to the states in the form of a block grant, a move that would have seriously undermined the intention to target vulnerable groups.

Congress and USDA have also resisted proposals to convert stamps to cash in the name of giving recipients more freedom over their household expenditure patterns.[6] Experiments have generally shown that food spending by recipients who receive straight cash assistance is less than what they would have spent with stamps. Yet problems of stigma and fraud associated with stamps have caused USDA to search for other means of providing broad access to conventional food sources. Since 1980 the department has sponsored several experiments with electronic benefit transfer cards, similar in appearance and function to the credit cards and debit cards with which increasing numbers of Americans purchase their groceries. Evaluations of the experiments indicate that all stakeholders—recipients, food stores, banks, and the public welfare agencies—find the cards more convenient, less stigmatizing, potentially less expensive to manage, and a better barrier to fraud than the paper stamps.[7] The 1996 welfare law mandates state adoption of electronic card systems by 2002.

What Needs to Be Done

Although the program fundamentals of the food assistance system are in place, food insecurity is still a significant problem. It is beginning to dawn on Washington that one shortcoming of federal food assistance programs is that they may be relatively blunt antidotes to food insecurity, averting it entirely for some households, yet failing to save others from chronic shortfalls. Now that the Current Population Survey has begun to provide data on the demographics of food insecurity and its relationship to participation in food assistance programs, it may be possible, however, for USDA to increase the efficiency of its array of programs through better targeting.

Increased funding of existing food assistance programs would also go a long way toward dealing with food insecurity. One potentially effective initiative would be to calibrate food stamps to the price of the Low Cost rather than the Thrifty Food Plan. Another would be to fund WIC as an entitlement. Neither of these is likely to attract broad support, however, even in an era of budget surpluses.

But if Americans are reluctant to commit to more expensive public solutions to hunger, they are not prepared to abandon the needy to their own devices. Most people feel a strong moral or religious obligation to help those in need. In response to these impulses Americans have invested substantial personal and financial resources in charitable feeding efforts. As we have seen, these are inadequate in a variety of ways and cannot compensate for the deficiencies of the system of public food programs. Nevertheless, it makes sense to tap the legitimacy, networks, resources, and broad-based acceptance of the charitable sector in addressing the hunger problem.

In the current political climate, one important key to making both the public and private systems of food assistance more effective is to strengthen the partnership between public and private actors in such a way that each legitimizes and fortifies the other.

Each of the modest reforms suggested below recognizes the unlikelihood of greatly increased funding of existing food assistance programs. Each is, therefore, comparatively inexpensive. In addition, each capitalizes on the growing interdependence of government and the nonprofit sector.[8]

The federal government must use the charitable feeding programs as vehicles for enrolling clients in public programs. We know that large numbers of people who use private food pantries and soup kitchens do not take advantage of federal food assistance programs. Reasons for nonparticipation vary, as we have seen, but Second Harvest figures suggest that more than 20 percent of its clients who are eligible for food stamps but who do not use them either do not know about the program or do not think it is worth the trouble to apply.[9] We also know that nonparticipation in public food assistance programs does not necessarily indicate a lack of need: the 1995 CPS survey found that 53.3 percent of those who could be classified as "food insecure with moderate hunger" received no food assistance from any federal program, nor did an astonishing 48.8 percent of those who fell in the "food insecure with severe hunger" category.[10] The survey analysis does not yet tell us who these people are or why they do not participate in food assistance programs. But it is difficult to believe that pride or the unwillingness to fill out application forms explains why those with severe hunger do not take advantage of federal food programs.

Publicly supported outreach programs have languished. But there are at least two ways to reach the reluctant and the uninformed short of educational campaigns and blanket mail or door-to-door contacts. One way would be to place public food assistance counselors in charitable food assistance agencies to provide information on all public feeding programs, make preliminary eligibility determinations, and begin the process of enrollment. Administrative costs could be minimized by focusing on large pantries and soup kitchens and by assigning the task of program intake to personnel already working in the county offices that distribute food stamps. Food assistance counselors would be performing functions at the street level that they are already performing in their offices. Since most pantries and soup kitchens are open only for limited hours and on certain days, on-site counselors would need to commit only a few hours a week. A second and cheaper way of reaching the unenrolled is to have charitable feeding agencies themselves collect names of non-participants in federal programs and forward those names to the local food stamp office for follow-up.

Government must use its resources to make private food assistance more effective. Federal and state governments must take steps to help charitable food agencies provide nutritionally balanced food supplies and to maintain their stocks. Most such actions are small, relatively inexpensive initiatives that would fill critical gaps in the operations of private food agencies. One step would be a federal or state program of grants-in-aid to county governments to hire nutritionists to serve food pantries and soup kitchens. Another would involve using federal commodity assistance programs, no longer used for reducing the surplus of the moment, to purchase perishable fruits and vegetables and high-protein foods that are seldom donated to food pantries or soup kitchens.

Commodity purchase programs should also operate countercyclically to take account of fluctuations over the course of the year in private donations. Yet another inexpensive program would provide grants-in-aid or low-interest loans to consortia of local food charities for shared refrigeration equipment, warehouse facilities, and trucks, all in chronic short supply in the private food assistance system.

The federal government must aggressively address the absence of supermarkets in poor areas by establishing stores in inner cities through public/private grocery partnerships. Poor people pay more for food than do middle-class consumers. A 1991 study by New York City's Department of Consumer Affairs found that low-income residents of the city paid about 8.8 percent more per year for groceries than those with incomes around the median, a difference that amounted to an additional outlay for poor people of about $350 annually.[11] A more extensive investigation of comparative grocery prices in ten metropolitan areas found on average that prices on a fixed basket of goods in inner city stores were slightly more than 4 percent higher than those in the suburbs. Warehouse grocery stores, found almost exclusively in suburban locales, were found to offer food at prices more than 13 percent below the national norm.[12]

A major source of the expenditure differences lies in the paucity of supermarkets in inner cities. Whereas one supermarket exists for every 5,800 people in Manhattan's middle-class neighborhoods on the Upper West Side, each supermarket in the heart of Brooklyn's minority ghetto serves 63,000.[13] Not only do smaller, high-price, low-volume stores tend to fill the interstices of the market, the few large stores that do exist rarely face price competition from other big stores.

Some urban economists point out that even though residents of inner-city neighborhoods are poor, they still represent a large, relatively untapped market.[14] Nonetheless, grocery stores face formidable costs in locating there. For example, insurance costs are substantially higher for stores in low-income areas. And operating in an environment in which consumers are both less well off and less likely to own cars means that few stores can anticipate the volume of activity that large suburban supermarkets generate. Thus inner city stores tend to be smaller and less able to take advantage of economies of scale.[15]

If poor people enjoyed access to the same competitive grocery market that middle-class consumers did, they would be able to get more food-purchasing mileage out of their existing food stamp allotment and cash expenditures. In other words access to a good grocery store would increase food acquisition without an increase in food stamps. One way to create a more competitive market is for the federal government to enter into partnerships with private grocery companies, either directly or through community-based organizations such as community development corporations.[16] By offering below-market loans for construction or building conversion, as well as access to a low-cost insurance pool, either to grocery chains or to new entrants into the supermarket business, public funds could offset some of the risks of doing business in the inner city. Financial assistance could be pegged at the point at which it reduced costs sufficiently to enable food pricing at some metropolitan mean. The maintenance of lower prices could be encouraged by spacing partnership grocery stores in the city in such a way as to create continuing competitive pressures.

Government and the grocery industry should subsidize transportation of poor consumers from home to supermarkets and back. Low-income consumers are less likely than better-off people to own cars. James McDonald and Paul Nelson found that while only 7.5 percent of suburban households lacked a car, 44 percent of the households were without in low-income zip codes in the ten central cities.[17] Lack of mobility obviously limits consumer search activity and comparison shopping.

Supermarkets are in any event rarely within easy walking distance. The average food stamp recipient in Detroit, for example, is .57 miles from the nearest high-volume grocery store, and nearly 10 percent of all food stamp households in that city are more than a mile away.[18] Carrying a week's worth of groceries on foot over such distances is difficult, so low-income shoppers who do not own cars use taxis or buses to shop. But the cost is high, involving outlays on transportation for grocery shopping of between $400 and $1,000 per year.[19]

Some cities, such as Pittsburgh, have experimented with subsidized van service from public housing projects to grocery stores, using federal Community Development Block Grant funds. Such a service would increase the food-buying capacity of poor people without increasing the cost of public food aid. Riders could even be charged a nominal fare and still come out ahead.

Just the two entities—government and riders—should not bear the entire cost of transportation subsidies. The private sector should be asked to share the cost. There is sufficient resource flexibility, even in the highly competitive grocery industry: we know, for example, that grocery stores are often willing to offer discounts to senior citizens and even to ordinary shoppers to encourage customer loyalty. In a similar vein, stores could be asked to help underwrite transportation services on the grounds that the vans bring new regular customers to the store.

Poverty, Food Insecurity, and Hunger

Ultimately, the remedy to hunger is to cure poverty. Not all poor people suffer from food insecurity, but almost all people classified as food insecure are poor. In the 1995 CPS study, 40.5 percent of those with incomes less than half the federal poverty line suffered some level of food insecurity, but only 3.8 percent of respondent households with incomes above 185 percent of the poverty line shared this condition. Food insecurity is also closely related to weekly cash expenditures for food. Among households that spend less than $20 per household member per week, nearly 20 percent report some degree of food insecurity; among households spending at least $40 per capita per week, the figure drops to just over 6 percent.[20]

Toward the end of its existence, the House select committee, like USDA, had also started to come to an understanding that people were hungry because they lacked the economic resources to guarantee regular access to food. Departing from its customary focus on strengthening the food assistance welfare system, the select committee had begun to organize hearings on "empowering" the poor through microcredit programs and various sorts of human capital investment accounts. If people could be helped along the road to economic self-sufficiency, the thinking went, perhaps by forming their own small businesses or investing in their own education, they would be less apt to be hungry.

Microcredit and similar ideas, though worthy, represent quite small and perhaps naively optimistic steps toward this complex goal, but the thinking behind them suggests that the select committee believed that the solutions to food deprivation lay finally in a household's economic autonomy derived from the decently remunerated work of some or one of its members. The idea is a sensible one, and it is one that is in the air. The welfare reform begun in 1996 was predicated on the same notion: work is the route to self-sufficiency. People who work will presumably not need food assistance. Food assistance programs, particularly food stamps, are to function only as a temporary safety net. People will earn their own keep.

Yet the idea that we can eliminate poverty if we insist that people work is finally unrealistic in the current climate: for one thing, we do not yet know how to keep people with few work or personal or social skills in the labor force. The verdict of the experiments that follow former welfare recipients into the workplace is that many do not stay long in a job. More important, there is not enough unskilled work to absorb all the poor. Even if there were enough jobs, those open to the poorest Americans would not pay wages that will buy enough food of the kind that people would wish to eat in order to eliminate food insecurity. But no plan to create jobs for the people coming off welfare or to absorb the unemployed on Indian reservations or in Appalachian hollows or in inner city wastelands is part of the welfare reform law that insists upon work.

Thus the problem and the potential for food insecurity remain. Economic self-sufficiency for all is a goal that cannot be achieved in a political climate that will not consider public job creation and an economic climate that maintains an earnings structure such that full-time work at the minimum wage produces an income below the poverty level. If this deeper and more enduring solution to hunger is beyond the capacity or imagination of American society at the close of the century, then we are left with the system of food assistance that we presently have. It remains underfunded, as the Hunger Has a Cure Act recognizes, but calling for more money is unlikely to produce results. The system can, however, be improved by strengthening nonprofit food charities, enrolling food pantry and soup kitchen users in public programs, and increasing the food purchasing power of existing food stamp allotments. These in the end are politically feasible, if less than optimal, steps. Enhanced in these ways, the food assistance currently provided by both public and private sources thus remains the most realistic and effective barrier to food insecurity for poor people in the United States.

Notes

Chapter 1

1. A Harris poll conducted at the end of 1986 found that 89 percent of a national sample believed that hunger in the United States was either a "very serious" problem (55 percent) or a "somewhat serious" problem (34 percent). This was up from 79 percent in a poll done two years earlier. Harris Poll, December 22, 1986. Figures released by the federal government are from Food and Consumer Service, *Household Food Security in the United States in 1995: Summary Report of the Food Security Measurement Project* (USDA, September 1997).

2. Food and Consumer Service, *Household Food Security*, p. 5. Surveyors did not determine if everyone in the household had actually experienced hunger, which was defined as "the uneasy or painful sensation caused by a lack of food. The recurrent and involuntary lack of access to food." The study distinguishes among those who are food insecure with moderate hunger (a household in which an adult is hungry) and those who experience severe hunger (a household in which a child is hungry).

3. Ibid, p. 37.

4. Linda Scott Kantor and others, *Estimating and Addressing America's Food Losses* (Economic Research Service, USDA, July 1997).

5. Bureau of the Census, *Statistical Abstract of the United States, 1997*, p. 853.

6. Ibid., p. 841.

7. Organization for Economic Cooperation and Development, *Food Consumption Statistics, 1979–1989* (Paris: OECD, 1991).

8. Food and Consumer Service, *Household Food Security in the United States in 1995*, p. 37.

9. Ibid., p. 45.

10. Ibid., p. 54.

11. *Congressional Record*, April 7, 1964, p. 7159.

12. Although a large, specialized literature exists on hunger measurement and on specific food assistance programs, there are no comprehensive scholarly treatments of hunger in America. Several books, now dated, were important in calling attention to the hunger problem, most notably Nick Kotz's *Let Them Eat Promises: The Politics of Hunger in America* (Prentice-Hall, 1969). See also Judith Segal, *Food for the Hungry: The Reluctant Society* (Johns Hopkins University Press, 1970). Ardith Maney has provided a detailed history of congressional and executive branch politics surrounding the development of several food assistance programs in *Still Hungry after All These Years: Food Assistance Policy from Kennedy to Reagan* (Greenwood, 1989).

13. Leo Marx, *The Machine in the Garden* (Oxford University Press, 1964), p. 75.

14. Quoted in Henry Nash Smith, *The Virgin Land* (Harvard University Press, 1950), p. 121.

15. Alexis de Tocqueville, *Democracy in America*, vol. 1 (Vintage, 1945), p. 331.

16. Arthur Guptill, *Norman Rockwell, Illustrator*, 3d ed. (New York: Watson-Guptill Publications, 1970), p. 140. A color plate of the painting is found on page 147.

17. David Potter, *People of Plenty* (University of Chicago Press, 1954), pp. 83–84.

18. *Congressional Record*, April 7, 1964, p. 7157.

19. Quoted in Julie Kosterlitz, "Beefing Up Food Stamps," *National Journal*, February 17, 1990, p. 391.

20. Text of the First Presidential Debate between John F. Kennedy and Richard Nixon, September 26, 1960. Reprinted in Sidney Kraus, ed., *The Great Debates* (Indiana University Press, 1962), p. 349.

21. Quoted in Elizabeth Drew, "Going Hungry in America," *Atlantic*, (December 1968), p. 58.

22. Richard Nixon, Message of the President to Congress, May 6, 1969, contained in *White House Conference on Food Nutrition and Health, Final Report* (1970).

23. *Report of the President's Task Force on Food Assistance* (January 1984), p. 2.

24. Janet Poppendieck, "Hunger and Public Action: A Social Problems Perspective," in Nancy Leidenfrost and Jennifer Wilkins, eds., *Food Security in the United States: A Guidebook for Public Issues Education* (Cooperative Extension, USDA, November 1994), p. 25.

25. Robert Shapiro and others, "The Polls: Public Assistance," *Public Opinion Quarterly*, vol. 51 (Spring 1987), p. 128.

26. A 1991 Penn and Schoen national survey found that 57 percent of the sample would be willing to pay $100 more in taxes to "fund a food program for every hungry child." A 1990 Roper poll found that 58 percent of a national sample would be willing to increase spending on nutrition programs, including food stamps and school lunch, even if taxes had to be increased. *American Public Opinion Index, 1969–1995* (CD-ROM).

27. This context is similar to what John Kingdon calls the "primeval soup" of policy ideas championed and contested by members of a broad "policy community." This community is composed of specialists in and out of government, which in the case of food assistance policy, mainly includes members of Congress and their staffs, researchers and program administrators at USDA, academic nutritionists, social scientists, and policy economists, and a wide range of activists from the anti-hunger interest and advocacy groups. Where I would extend Kingdon's model is to suggest that the policy ideas swirling around in the soup include fundamental issues of definition as well as alternative proposals about how to address the problem. What emerges from this policy debate, as Kingdon argues, is constrained finally by what is acceptable to the public. John Kingdon, *Agendas, Alternatives, and Public Policies* (Scott, Foresman, 1984), pp. 122–24, 146.

Chapter 2

1. The following exchange between Representative Robin Tallon (D-S.C.) and a witness before the House is illustrative:

> Rep. Tallon: I wonder if there is a medical definition for hunger. . . .
> Could you speak to that subject, please, sir?
> Dr. Kleinman: Mr. Chairman, I don't know of a good definition for hunger except you know it when you see it or see somebody suffering from it.

This appears in *Hunger in America, Its Effects on Children and Families, and Implications for the Future*, Hearing before the Subcommittee on Domestic Marketing, Consumer Relations, and Nutrition of the House Committee on Agriculture, 102 Cong. 1 sess. (Government Printing Office, May 8, 1991), p. 69.

2. Barbara Cohen and Martha Burt, *Eliminating Hunger: Food Security Policy for the 1990s* (Urban Institute, 1989), p. 3; see also J. Larry Brown, "Hunger in the U.S.," *Scientific American*, vol. 256 (February 1987), p. 37.

3. John Kingdon makes a similar point in *Agendas, Alternatives, and Public Policies* (Scott, Foresman, 1984), pp. 98, 103.

4. David Dery, *Problem Definition in Policy Analysis* (University Press of Kansas, 1984), pp. xii, 5.

5. Roger Cobb and Charles Elder, *Participation in American Politics: The Dynamics of Agenda-Building*, 2d ed. (Johns Hopkins University Press, 1983), p. 174.

6. Contrast Linda Neuhauser's definition of food security as hinging on the ability to consume "nutritionally adequate" food through normal food channels with the widely used Radimer/Cornell Food Insecurity measure that defines food insecurity as "the inability to acquire or consume an adequate quality or sufficient quantity of food in socially acceptable ways, or the uncertainty that one will be able to do so." See Neuhauser's testimony in *Food Security and Methods of Assessing Hunger in the United States*, Hearing before the House Select Committee on Hunger, 101 Cong. 1 sess. (GPO, March 23, 1989), p. 46. The Radimer definition is contained, among other places, in Anne Kendall and others, *Validation of the Radimer/Cornell Hunger and Food Insecurity Measures*, Final Project Report (Division of Nutritional Sciences, Cornell University, May 1994), p. 1. The same issue—whether or not to include nutritional criteria in food security measures—cropped up among the members of the working group developing final scales from the Current Population Survey of hunger prevalence conducted in the spring of 1995, according to a USDA official who wished to remain anonymous (discussion with the author, Washington, D.C., May 8, 1996).

7. This is a concern, for example, of John Cook and J. Larry Brown of the Tufts Center on Hunger, Poverty and Nutrition Policy. See their "Development of a Baseline Hunger Measure: A Synthesis of Critical Issues" (Medford, Mass.: Tufts University School of Nutrition, January 20, 1994), pp. 9, 11.

8. The point is made in a "fact sheet" on the 1991 Freedom from Want Act, sponsored by Representative Tony Hall (D-Ohio): "There is . . . a need for a commonly accepted formula for quantifying hunger problems in the U.S. and distinguishing chronic hunger problems from those that occur in other countries" (mimeo, files of the House Select Committee on Hunger, May 13, 1991).

9. Lester Brown's comment on the international food crisis is typical of the scarcity perspective: "Looking at the world of the early seventies, one is struck with the sobering realization that it appears to be losing its capacity to feed itself. . . . Currently the resources used to expand food production—land, water, energy, fertilizer—are all scarce." "The Complexity of the Food Problem," in Sartaj Aziz, ed., *Hunger, Politics and Markets* (New York University Press, 1975), p. 11. Even as Americans were forging a sociological understanding of domestic hunger, however, those concerned with hunger elsewhere in the world still focused on the physiology of food deprivation. For example, the Hunger Project, a food advocacy organization, defines "countries in which hunger exists as a basic, society-wide issue as those with an infant mortality rate above 50 per 1,000 live births." The Hunger Project, *Ending Hunger: An Idea Whose Time Has Come* (Praeger, 1985), p. 17. The U.S. infant mortality rate in the early 1990s was around 9 per 1,000 live births.

10. Judith Segal suggests that the precipitating event in the emergence of hunger as a visible issue occurred in the winter of 1966 when Representative Joseph Resnick (D-N.Y.) toured Mississippi and witnessed the devastating poverty of black sharecroppers displaced by agricultural mechanization. Judith Segal, *Food for the Hungry* (Johns Hopkins University Press, 1970), pp. 9–10. In fact Resnick's subsequent letters to administration officials and congressional leaders elicited little news coverage and less government response. A more appropriate beginning is the well-documented visit to the delta region by Robert Kennedy.

11. *Hunger and Malnutrition,* Hearings before the Subcommittee on Employment, Manpower, and Poverty of the Senate Committee on Labor and Public Welfare, 90 Cong. 1 sess. (GPO, July 11–12, 1967), pp. 1–2.

12. Michael Latham, a professor at Cornell University, remarked in testimony before Congress that "for me, a physician who has dealt with a great deal of kwashiorkor and nutritional marasmus in Africa, it was certainly eye opening to sit in a comfortable U.S. home and to see cases of these extremely serious nutritional diseases displayed in Texas and Arizona." *Nutrition and Human Needs,* Hearings before the Senate Select Committee on Nutrition and Human Needs, 90 Cong. 2 sess. (GPO, December 17–19, 1968), p. 43.

13. Hunger counties included all those in which the postneonatal mortality rate was at least twice as high as the national average and in which the percentage of the population below the poverty line was also twice the national average. Citizens' Board of Inquiry into Hunger and Malnutrition in the United States, *Hunger, U.S.A.* (Beacon Press, 1968), p. 38.

14. Text of the CBS script is contained in *Hunger and Malnutrition in the United States,* Hearings before the Senate Subcommittee on Employment, Manpower, and Poverty, 90 Cong. 2 sess. (GPO, May 23, 29; June 12, 14, 1968), p. 60.

15. Ibid., p. 61.

16. Ibid., pp. 7–8.

17. *Nutrition and Human Needs,* Hearings, pp. 42–43.

18. *The Food Gap: Poverty and Malnutrition in the United States,* Interim Report of the Senate Select Committee on Nutrition and Human Needs (GPO, August 1969), p. 8.

19. White House Conference on Food, Nutrition and Health, *Final Report* (GPO, 1970), p. 46.

20. *Hunger–1973,* Report prepared by the staff of the Senate Select Committee on Nutrition and Human Needs (GPO, May 1973), p. 8 (emphasis added).

21. Ibid., p. 1.

22. Senate hearings in 1979 designed to assess progress toward the elimination of hunger were studded with references to hunger and malnutrition, but many of those who testified were doctors who had originally visited Appalachia and the Mississippi Delta in 1967 and 1968 on fact-finding trips. See, for example, the remarks of Drs. Raymond Wheeler (pp. 9–10) and Gordon Harper

(p. 41) in *Hunger in America: Ten Years Later*, Hearing before the Subcommittee on Nutrition of the Senate Agriculture Committee, 96 Cong. 1 sess. (GPO, April 30, 1979).

23. William Boehm, Paul Nelson, and Kathryn Longen, *Progress toward Eliminating Hunger in America*, Agricultural Economic Report no. 446 (USDA, January 1980), p. 3.

24. *Food Security and Methods of Assessing Hunger in the United States*, Hearing before the House Select Committee on Hunger, 101 Cong. 1 sess. (GPO, March 23, 1989), p. 40.

25. *Nutrition and Health*, Committee Print, Senate Select Committee on Nutrition and Human Needs, 94 Cong. 1 sess. (GPO, December 1975), p. 56. The statement was drafted in 1972. Another (later) version of the access goal is contained in *Towards a National Nutrition Policy*, Committee Print, Senate Select Committee on Nutrition and Human Needs, 94 Cong. 1 sess. (GPO, May 1975), p. 62.

26. *Report of the President's Task Force on Food Assistance* (January 1984), p. 36.

27. Ibid.

28. Ibid., p. 39.

29. According to Barbara Cohen, the food security definition was refined in meetings that included Sheldon Margen, Cathy Campbell, Martha Burt, Linda Neuhauser, and herself. Interview with Barbara Cohen, December 8, 1993.

30. R. P. Sharma, *Approaches to Monitoring Access to Food and Household Food Security* (Rome: FAO Committee on World Food Security, 17 sess., March 23–27, 1992).

31. *Food Security and Methods of Assessing Hunger in the United States*, Hearing, p. 41.

32. Cohen and Burt, *Eliminating Hunger: Food Security Policy for the 1990s*. These writers insist that hunger is the process "of being unable to obtain a nutritionally adequate diet from non-emergency food channels" (p. 4). Others who have adopted the notion of food security see hunger as a state of being.

33. House Select Committee on Hunger, *Food Security in the United States*, Committee Report (GPO, October 1990), p. 3.

34. Ibid., p. 2.

35. The point is made by Margen in *Food Security and Methods of Assessing Hunger in the United States*, Hearing, p. 39.

36. Ibid., pp. 5, 19. The concept of a fundamental right to food security also appears in the text of an omnibus hunger assistance bill, entitled the Freedom from Want Act. Introduced by Representatives Tony Hall (D-Ohio) and Bill Emerson (R-Mo.), who were colleagues on the House Select Committee on Hunger, in the spring of 1991, H.R. 2258 was referred to half a dozen standing committees. It eventually died in committee(s). The term "food security" also appears in legislation passed by Congress in 1985. P.L. 99-198 is in fact entitled

the Food Security Act of 1985. In this law, however, "food security" has not yet taken on the narrow meaning employed by the nutrition community to denote the absence of hunger. The term refers instead to an "abundance of food and fiber at reasonable prices" for all "consumers." The bill seeks to ensure such abundance by extending and revising agricultural price supports, agricultural export policies, farm credit, resource conservation, and food assistance to low-income persons.

Chapter 3

1. Kathy Radimer, Christine Olson, and Cathy Campbell, "Development of Indicators to Assess Hunger," *Journal of Nutrition*, vol. 120 (November 1990), p. 1545.

2. Citizens' Board of Inquiry into Hunger and Malnutrition in the United States, *Hunger, U.S.A.* (Beacon Press, 1968), p. 32.

3. *Nutrition and Human Needs*, Hearings before the Senate Select Committee on Nutrition and Human Needs, 90 Cong. 2 sess. (GPO, December 17–19, 1968), p. 42.

4. It was on this trip that Senator George Murphy (D-Calif.) said, "I didn't know that we were going to be dealing with the situation of starving people and starving youngsters." Quoted in Physician Task Force on Hunger in America, *Hunger in America* (Wesleyan University Press, 1985), p. ix.

5. *Report of the President's Task Force on Food Assistance* (January 1984), p. 37. The Physician Task Force on Hunger in America makes a virtually identical comment in its report, *Hunger in America*, p. 183.

6. Letter from J. Larry Brown to Representative Tony Hall, chair, House Select Committee on Hunger, September 8, 1992. Copy supplied to the author.

7. Jean-Pierre Habicht and Linda Meyers, "Principles for Effective Surveys of Hunger and Malnutrition in the United States," *Journal of Nutrition*, vol. 121 (March 1991), p. 405.

8. Food and Consumer Service, *Household Food Security in the United States in 1995: Summary Report of the Food Security Measurement Project* (USDA, September 1997), p. 45.

9. Interagency Board for Nutrition Monitoring and Related Research, *Third Report on Nutrition Monitoring in the United States: Executive Summary* (December 1995), p. ES-19. Respondents were asked the standard food sufficiency question.

10. Beth Osborne Daponte, "Private versus Public Relief: Utilization of Food Pantries versus Food Stamps among Poor Households in Allegheny, County, Pennsylvania," Discussion Paper 1091–96 (Institute for Research on Poverty, University of Wisconsin–Madison, 1996), p. 23.

11. Ibid.

12. *Report of the President's Task Force on Food Assistance*, p. 38.

13. For example, the U.S. Conference of Mayors survey of hunger in selected cities asks in its questionnaire only for trends in "the total number of requests for emergency food assistance in your city." U.S. Conference of Mayors, *A Status Report on Hunger and Homelessness in America's Cities: 1992* (Washington, D.C.: USCM, December 1992), appendix. Other surveys of demand are more careful to distinguish the number of requests from the number of clients. A national survey sponsored by Second Harvest asks agencies about the number of "unduplicated clients." Second Harvest, *1993 National Research Study* (Chicago: Second Harvest, March 1994).

14. Radimer, Olson, and Campbell, "Development of Indicators to Assess Hunger." See also Ronette Briefel and Catherine Woteki, "Development of Food Sufficiency Questions for the Third National Health and Nutrition Examination Survey," *Journal of Nutrition Education*, vol. 24 (January/February Supplement, 1992), pp. 24S–28S.

15. Radimer, Olson, and Campbell, "Development of Indicators to Assess Hunger," pp. 1544–47.

16. *Food Security and Methods of Assessing Hunger in the United States.* Hearing before the House Select Committee on Hunger, 101 Cong. 1 sess. (GPO, March 23, 1989), p. 153.

17. Ibid., p. 40. See the comments of Sheldon Margen of the School of Public Health, University of California, Berkeley.

18. For example, "Dr. David Steinman provided the Board with studies showing that six-year-olds from Appalachia were one to two inches shorter than national (Boston-Iowa) norms." And "The Board during its field trip to Boston received a report of a comprehensive biochemical dietary study of low income children conducted by the faculty of the Harvard School of Public Health." Citizens' Board of Inquiry, *Hunger, U.S.A.*, pp. 20, 21.

19. Ibid., p. 16.

20. Ibid., p. 32. This figure is based on data that show that about a third of people below the poverty line suffered from some sign of malnutrition. Twenty-nine million people were below the poverty line, which yielded the estimate of 10 million (p. 32).

21. *The Food Gap: Poverty and Malnutrition in the United States*, Interim Report of the Senate Select Committee on Nutrition and Human Needs, 91 Cong. 1 sess. (GPO, August 1969).

22. Ibid., pp. 20, 21.

23. Ibid., p. 20.

24. Ibid.

25. Ibid. (emphasis added).

26. This brief history is contained in U.S. Department of Health, Education, and Welfare, *Ten-State Nutrition Survey, 1968–1970*, vol. 1, Historical Development (Atlanta: Center for Disease Control, 1972), pp. I-1–I-2.

27. Quoted in *Towards a National Nutrition Policy*, Senate Senate Select Committee on Nutrition and Human Needs, Committee Print, 94 Cong. 1 sess. (GPO, May 1975), p. 12.

28. The story of the politics of the survey is told in *Nutrition and Health*, Committee Print, Senate Select Committee on Nutrition and Human Needs, 94 Cong. 1 sess. (GPO, December 1975), pp. 39–40. In capsule form, the account here holds that the Nixon administration was angered by the outspoken study director, Dr. Arnold Schaefer, who decried the presence of large numbers of undernourished poor in affluent America and characterized existing federal food assistance programs as "damned ineffective." The Center for Disease Control is described by the Senate select committee as "the burial site for the Ten-State Survey" (p. 42). Schaefer's testimony is contained in *Nutrition and Human Needs–1970*, Hearing before the Senate Select Committee on Nutrition and Human Needs, 91 Cong. 2 sess. (GPO, April 27, 1970), p. 776.

29. The Partnership for Health Act Amendments of 1967 had called for a report within six months of the passage of the bill. The report was published in 1972.

30. Department of Health, Education, and Welfare, *Ten-State Nutrition Survey, 1969–1970*, vol. 3, Clinical (Atlanta: Center for Disease Control, 1972), p. III-1.

31. *Nutrition and Human Needs–1970*, Hearing, p. 769.

32. See, for example, the summary of the doctors' findings and the exchange between Senator McGovern and Dr. Raymond Wheeler in *Hunger in America: Ten Years Later*, Hearing before the Subcommittee on Nutrition of the Senate Agriculture Committee, 96 Cong. 1 sess. (GPO, April 30, 1979), p. 21.

33. The witness was Dr. J. Michael McGinnis, deputy assistant secretary for Health, Disease Prevention, and Health Promotion, Public Health Service. *Food Security and Methods of Assessing Hunger in the United States*, Hearing, pp. 85–86.

34. These objectives are laid out in numerous reports of the survey. See, for example, USDA, Human Nutrition and Information Service, *Food Consumption: Households in the United States, Spring, 1977*, Report H-1 (1982), p. 5.

35. Judith Segal, *Food for the Hungry: The Reluctant Society* (Johns Hopkins University Press, 1970), pp. 15–16.

36. Ibid.

37. Interview with Mary Hama, economist, Human Nutrition and Information Service, USDA, July 27, 1994.

38. See table 27 in USDA, *Food Consumption: Households in the United States, Seasons and Year 1977–78*, p. 294.

39. Confidential communication to the author, July 27, 1994.

40. Donald Rose, Peter Basiotis, and Bruce Klein, "Improving Federal Efforts to Assess Hunger and Food Insecurity," *Food Review*, vol. 18 (January–April 1995), p. 20.

41. Sharron Cristofar and Peter Basiotis, "Dietary Intakes and Selected Characteristics of Women Ages 19–50 and Their Children Ages 1–5 Years by Reported Perception of Food Sufficiency," *Journal of Nutrition Education*, vol. 24 (March–April 1992), pp. 53–58.

42. According to Jennifer Wolch and Michael Dear, estimates of the number of homeless (not all of whom are hungry, of course) range from 350,000 to 3 million. *Malign Neglect* (Jossey-Bass, 1993), p. 31.

43. The range is derived by multiplying the percentage saying their households have insufficient food by the total number of households in the United States for 1980, 1985, and 1990. Then for each of those years the resulting number of households is multiplied by the average number of people per household. Data on the number of households and average size are contained in Bureau of the Census, *Statistical Abstract of the United States, 1990*, p. 45, and the same publication for 1993, p. 59.

44. J. Larry Brown cites a survey by the Food Research and Action Center of 300 emergency food programs around the country, for example. "Hunger in the U.S.," *Scientific American*, vol. 256 (February 1987), p. 37. Barbara Cohen and Martha Burt write, "Other than a few questions included in national food and health surveys, all hunger studies are conducted at local levels, usually by community groups." *Eliminating Hunger: Food Security Policy for the 1990s* (Urban Institute, October 1989), p. 5. A notable exception to the community group studies is a report by the Government Accounting Office detailing rising levels of activity among food pantries and soup kitchens in Baltimore, Washington, D.C., and several other sites. A typical finding is that whereas the Maryland Food Bank distributed 30,000 pounds of food a month when it opened in 1979, it was distributing 220,000 pounds per month by 1982. Government Accounting Office, *Public and Private Efforts to Feed America's Poor* (GPO, June 23, 1983), p. 6.

45. Marion Nestle and Sally Gutmacher, "Hunger in the United States: Rationale, Methods, and Policy Implications of State Hunger Surveys," *Journal of Nutrition Education*, vol. 24 (1992), p. 18S.

46. Cohen and Burt, *Eliminating Hunger*, pp. 11–14.

47. These are listed in USCM, *A Status Report on Hunger and Homelessness in America's Cities*, pp. 5–6.

48. USCM, "Mayors' Annual Survey Finds Continued Growth in Demand for Emergency Food and Shelter," Press release, December 19, 1995. In 1995, 72 percent of the cities registered an increase.

49. Second Harvest, *1993 National Research Study*.

50. Surveyors did ask food service clients several questions that appear in question sets used sometimes to ascertain "food security" status. For example, clients were asked "How often do you worry about where your next meal is coming from . . . ?" Nearly 28 percent answered "never." Almost 89 percent reported that their children had not missed any meals in the past month because there was

not enough money or food, and 71 percent of adults said that they themselves had not had to miss meals either. Second Harvest, *1993 National Research Study*, pp.160–63. These results suggest that the emergency client pool is not exactly coincident with the "food insecure" population.

51. In hearings before the House of Representatives, Representative Leon Panetta (D-Calif.) asked the executive director of the Food Research and Action Center, Robert Fersh, if there had been any comparable study before the CCHIP effort. Fersh replied that there were no comparable studies and that "experts in the field view this as a benchmark study." *Hunger in America, Its Effects on Children and Families, and Implications for the Future*, Hearing before the Subcommittee on Domestic Marketing, Consumer Relations, and Nutrition of the House Committee on Agriculture, 102 Cong. 1 sess. (GPO, May 8, 1991), p. 74. The CCHIP questionnaire was developed and tested by Cheryl Wehler prior to its implementation by FRAC. See Cheryl Wehler, Richard Ira Scott, and Jennifer Anderson, "The Community Childhood Hunger Identification Project: A Model of Domestic Hunger—Demonstration Project in Seattle, Washington," *Journal of Nutrition Education*, vol. 24 (January–February 1992). On the importance of the CCHIP questionnaire to the development of the federal NHANES III instrument, see Ronette Briefel and Catherine Woteki, "Development of Food Sufficiency Questions for the Third National Health and Nutrition Examination Survey," *Journal of Nutrition Education*, vol. 24 (January–February Supplement, 1992), p. 25S. CCHIP was also important for the development of the battery of questions for the Census Bureau's Current Population Survey supplement. Interview with Bruce Klein, Food and Nutrition Service, USDA, July 21, 1994.

52. Wehler, Scott, and Anderson, "The Community Childhood Hunger Identification Project," p. 29S.

53. Ibid.

54. Each affirmative answer was followed by questions that ask whether the experience occurred in the last twelve months or the last thirty days and then how many days in the last year or month the household suffered the particular deprivation. Overall, the survey results found that families experiencing hunger do so about seven days per month and during at least six months of the year. Food Research and Action Center, *Community Childhood Hunger Identification Project* (FRAC, March 1991), p. 12.

55. The seven areas included Suffolk County, New York; Pontiac; Hartford; and Hennepin County, Minnesota; and three rural counties in California, Alabama, and Florida. A total of 2,335 low-income families were covered by the surveys. The CCHIP formula has since been replicated in a number of states. Larry Brown counts eleven different surveys in nine states conducted between 1992 and 1994. Letter from J. Larry Brown to the author, January 29, 1996.

56. NHANES I was conducted between 1971 and 1974; NHANES II took place from 1976 to 1980.

57. Unpublished data supplied by USDA's Human Nutrition Information Service in a personal communication to the author, July 27, 1994.

58. See, for example, Christine Olson, Edward Frongillo, and Ann Kendall, "Validation of Measures for Estimating the Prevalence of Hunger and Food Insecurity in the Current Population Survey Module: A Combination of Cornell and CCHIP Items," paper presented at USDA Conference on Food Security Measurement and Research, January 21–22, 1994.

59. Food and Consumer Service, *Household Food Security in the United States in 1995*, pp. E-2–E-3.

60. See, for example, Foodchain, "U.S. Hunger Facts," n.d.; Bread for the World Institute, *Hunger 1995* (Silver Spring, Md., 1994), p.16; National Student Campaign Against Hunger and Homelessness, *Fall Organizing Manual, 1994–95*, p. 10; World Hunger Year, *Just The Facts*, n.d.; Share Our Strength, "Hunger Today: The Worldwide Crisis Continues," fact sheet, n.d. (Share Our Strength cites a figure of 20 million.) The source of the 30 million figure is the Tufts Center on Hunger, Poverty, and Nutrition Policy. The data sources and the derivation of the estimates are described in "Estimating the Number of Hungry Americans," Draft Research in Progress Working Paper, DHPNP-WP HE01-090292 (Medford, Mass.: Tufts University School of Nutrition, 1992). The estimates were reported to the chair of the select committee, Representative Tony Hall, in a letter from J. Larry Brown, director of the center, September 8, 1992.

Chapter 4

1. See, for example, Secretary of the Treasury William Simon's remarks in *Food Stamp Program*, Hearings before the House Committee on Agriculture, 94 Cong. 1 sess. (GPO, January–April 1976), p. 44.

2. The Agricultural Research, Extension, and Education Act of 1998 restores eligibility to certain categories of legal immigrants, including children under the age of eighteen, disabled adults, people who were over sixty-five at the time the 1996 welfare reform bill was passed, and Hmong immigrants. These groups account for approximately 250,000 of the 900,000 legal immigrants removed from the food stamp rolls by the Personal Responsibility and Work Opportunity Reconciliation Act of 1996.

3. See in particular, James Ohls and Harold Beebout, *The Food Stamp Program* (Urban Institute, 1993); Maurice MacDonald, *Food, Stamps, and Income Maintenance* (Academic Press, 1977); Ardith Maney, *Still Hungry after All These Years: Food Assistance Policy from Kennedy to Reagan* (Greenwood, 1989); Jeffrey Berry, *Feeding Hungry People* (Rutgers University Press, 1984); and John Ferejohn, "Logrolling in an Institutional Context: A Case Study of Food Stamp Legislation,"

in Gerald Wright Jr., Leroy Rieselbach, and Lawrence Dodd, eds., *Congress and Policy Change* (New York: Agathon Press, 1986), pp. 223–53.

4. Executive Order 10914, January 24, 1961. See *CIS Index to Presidential Executive Orders and Proclamations* (Congressional Information Service, 1986).

5. Presidential Message to Congress on Economic Recovery and Growth, February 2, 1961. *Congressional Record,* February 2, 1961, p. 1677.

6. The most thorough legislative history of the food stamp program is Randall B. Ripley, "Legislative Bargaining and the Food Stamp Act, 1964," in Frederic Cleaveland, ed., *Congress and Urban Problems* (Brookings, 1969), pp. 279–310.

7. Consumers Union, *Hunger, the Food Stamp Program, and State Discretion* (Washington, D.C.: Consumers Union, July 1995), pp. 6–8.

8. *Food Stamps: The Statement of Hon. William E. Simon, Secretary of the Treasury, with a Staff Analysis,* Committee Print, Senate Select Committee on Nutrition and Human Needs, 94 Cong. 1 sess. (GPO, December 1975), p. 42.

9. Calculation of the gross income is complex. It excludes or disregards a variety of sources of cash income (for example, Pell grants). Net income must not exceed the poverty line, but this is calculated by permitting a variety of deductions from gross income.

10. Carole Trippe, Pat Doyle, and Andrew Asher, *Trends in Food Stamp Program Participation Rates: 1976 to 1990* (Food and Nutrition Service, USDA, July 1992), p. 24.

11. Ibid., p. 43.

12. *1996 Green Book,* Committee Print, House Committee on Ways and Means, 104 Cong. 2 sess. (GPO, 1996), p. 874.

13. Ibid., p. 880.

14. Bureau of the Census, *Statistical Abstract of the United States, 1997,* p. 376.

15. Ferejohn, "Logrolling in an Institutional Context." See also Ohls and Beebout, *The Food Stamp Program,* p. 128.

16. Barbara Claffey and Thomas Stuckey, "The Food Stamp Program," in Don Hadwiger and Ross Talbot, eds., *Food Policy and Farm Programs* (New York: Academy of Political Science, 1982), p. 41. They quote a 1940 USDA report on food stamps which asserts that "the principal objective is to raise farmers' incomes by increasing the demand for their products and to so use food surpluses as to improve the diet of undernourished families in this country."

17. William Boehm, Paul Nelson, and Kathryn Longen, *Progress toward Eliminating Hunger in America,* Agricultural Economic Report 446 (USDA, January 1980), p. 6.

18. Janet Poppendieck, "Policy, Advocacy, and Justice: The Case of Food Assistance Reform," in David Gil and Eva Gil, eds., *Toward Social and Economic Justice* (Cambridge, Mass.: Schenkman, 1985), p. 105.

19. Janet Poppendieck, *Breadlines Knee-Deep in Wheat* (Rutgers University Press, 1986), pp. 177, 200.

20. Ibid., p. 200.

21. See, for example, the comments of Representative Donald Rosenthal (D-N.Y.), *Congressional Record*, April 7, 1964, p. 7138.

22. Ibid., p. 7136.

23. Remarks of Representative William Ryan (D-N.Y.), ibid., pp. 7157–58.

24. *The Food Stamp Controversy of 1975: Background Materials*, Committee Print, Senate Select Committee on Nutrition and Human Needs, 94 Cong. 1 sess. (GPO, October 1975), pp. 21–25. More recently, Ohls and Beebout have estimated that each additional dollar of food stamp aid increases food expenditures by about 25 cents. Although the program clearly increases total spending on food, the authors find this impact disappointingly small. *The Food Stamp Program*, p. 102.

25. Ripley, "Legislative Bargaining and the Food Stamp Act," pp. 294–95.

26. *Congressional Record*, April 7, 1964, pp. 7153–54.

27. Ibid, p. 7126.

28. *Mississippi Revisited: Poverty and Hunger Problems and Prospects*, Hearing before the House Select Committee on Hunger, 102 Cong. 1 sess. (GPO, May 3, 1991), p. 26.

29. *Hunger in America, Its Effects on Children and Families, and Implications for the Future*, Hearing before the House Subcommittee on Domestic Marketing, Consumer Relations, and Nutrition of the House Committee on Agriculture, 102 Cong. 1 sess. (GPO, May 8, 1991), p. 2.

30. Ibid., pp. 15, 60. See also testimony on pp. 77–79.

31. *Food Assistance in Rural Communities: Problems, Prospects, and Ideas from Urban Programs*, Hearing before the House Select Committee on Hunger, 102 Cong. 1 sess. (GPO, April 5, 1991), p. 6.

32. *Hunger in America*, Hearing, pp. 74–75.

33. *Congressional Record*, December 16, 1970, p. 41985.

34. Ohls and Beebout, *The Food Stamp Program*, p. 161.

35. Comments of Catherine Bertini, then assistant secretary, Food and Consumer Service, USDA, in *Food Stamp Trafficking and the Food Stamp Electronic Benefit Transfer Program*, Joint Hearing before the Subcommittee on Policy Research and Insurance of the House Committee on Banking, Finance, and Urban Affairs, the Subcommittee on Regulation, Business Opportunities and Energy of the House Committee on Small Business, and the Subcommittee on Domestic Marketing, Consumer Relations, and Nutrition of the House Committee on Agriculture, 102 Cong. 2 sess. (GPO, March 15, 1992), p. 33.

36. On Depression-era suspicions, see Berry, *Feeding Hungry People*, p. 22.

37. Clayton Yeutter, assistant secretary of USDA during the Nixon administration, commenting on fraud and abuse, observed that the issue "constantly arises,

particularly from critics of the program who seek means by which it may be casti-
gated or indicted." *Federal Food Programs–1973*, Hearing before the Senate Select
Committee on Nutrition and Human Needs, 93 Cong. 1 sess. (GPO, June 4,
1973), p. 198. Representative Frederick Richmond (D-N.Y.) made a similar observation in hearings in 1981: "There are many, many people in this country—and
unfortunately some of them are members of this Congress—who believe that food
stamps are bad in principle. When these people see the outright fraud and administrative neglect that allows millions of dollars to be literally stolen, they use the
facts of fraud and abuse as leverage to attack the entire food stamp program."
Fraud in the Food Stamp Program, Hearing before the Subcommittee on Domestic
Marketing, Consumer Relations, and Nutrition of the House Committee on
Agriculture, 97 Cong. 1 sess. (GPO, September 22, 1981), p. 1.

38. Representative Harley Staggers (D-W.V.) once astutely remarked that "in
this program, it's easy to take offense at a relatively low number [of fraud cases]."
Food Stamp Trafficking and the Food Stamp Electronic Benefit Transfer Program,
Hearing, p. 37.

39. *Enforcement of the Food Stamp Program*, Hearing before the House
Committee on Agriculture, 104 Cong. 1 sess. (GPO, February 1, 1995).

40. As table 4-2 shows, between 1974 and 1975 average monthly participation in the program went from just over 12.8 million to 16.3 million. Unemployment rose to 8.9 percent, and the cost of food increased sharply. See also Berry,
Feeding Hungry People, pp. 81–82.

41. One estimate was that unmarried students comprised less than 1 percent
of all participants. *Food Stamps: The Statement of Hon. William E. Simon*, p. 102. A
study conducted by the General Accounting Office that examined food stamp use
among students at six universities around the country found that 3.76 percent of all
students were enrolled in the program, a figure skewed upward by the fact that
more than 60 percent of the participants came from just one school, San Francisco
State University. Only about 6 percent of a sample of the student food stamp recipients from all six schools received financial support from parents. GAO, *Student
Participation in the Food Stamp Program at Six Selected Universities*, Report to the
House Committee on Agriculture (April 1976), pp. 4, 6. For amendments introduced see, for example, *Congressional Record*, December 16, 1970, pp. 41979,
41980, 41984; May 15, 1973, p. 15763; July 15, 1975, p. 22896. See also *Food
Stamp Program*, Hearings before the House Committee on Agriculture, 93 Cong.
1 sess (GPO, March 13, 1973), p. 14; and *Food Stamp Regulation Proposals*,
Hearings before the House Committee on Agriculture, 94 Cong. 1 sess. (GPO,
January 30, 1975), p. 2.

42. Senator Herman Talmadge (D-Ga.) supported amendments to the Food
Stamp Act in 1976 that he said would "eliminate affluent families from the food
stamp program." *Congressional Record*, April 5, 1976, p. 9383.

43. *Congressional Record*, July, 15, 1975, p. 22896.

44. *Food Stamp Program*, Hearings before the Subcommittee on Domestic Marketing, Consumer Relations, and Nutrition of the House Committee on Agriculture, 96 Cong. 1 sess. (GPO, October 10, 17, 18, 30, 31, November 1, 1979), p. 157.

45. *Options for Reforming the Food Stamp Program*, Hearing before the Senate Select Committee on Nutrition and Human Needs, 94 Cong. 1 sess. (GPO, July 31, 1975), p. 52. Statistics on net income eligibility for 1975 are reported in MacDonald, *Food, Stamps, and Income Maintenance*, p. 27.

46. This was Secretary William Simon's accusation. *The Food Stamp Controversy of 1975*, Committee Print, p. 36.

47. "Food Stamps: Out of Control," *U.S. News and World Report*, vol. 79 (September 1, 1975), pp. 12–13.

48. *Federal Food Programs–1973*, Hearings, p. 233.

49. GAO, *The Food Stamp Program—Overissued Benefits Not Recovered and Fraud Not Punished*, Report to Congress (GPO, July 18, 1977), pp. ii–iii.

50. GAO, *Food Assistance: Reducing Fraud and Abuse in the Food Stamp Program with Electronic Benefit Transfer Technologies* (GPO, February 2, 1994), p. 3.

51. *Food Stamp Trafficking and the Food Stamp Electronic Benefit Transfer Program*, Hearing, p. 8.

52. *Enforcement of the Food Stamp Program*, Hearing, pp. 5, 17.

53. *Congressional Record*, February 9, 1976, p. 2900; *Enforcement of the Food Stamp Program*, Hearing, p. 5.

54. *The Food Stamp Controversy of 1975*, Committee Print, p. 43.

55. *Fraud in the Food Stamp Program*, Hearing, p. 5.

56. Robert Fersh, director of the Food Research and Action Center, praised Congress at the close of hearings on food stamp trafficking. "This has been an extraordinarily positive hearing . . . extraordinarily effective in putting into perspective where the real problems lie, and a hearing that we feared might become one that the press would use to take off on beating the food stamp program down." *Food Stamp Trafficking and the Food Stamp Electronic Benefit Transfer Program*, Hearings, p. 53.

57. See the letter from Edward Golob, director of a relief agency in Johnstown, Pennsylvania, *Congressional Record*, April 7, 1964, p. 7141.

58. Berry, *Feeding Hungry People*, p. 29.

59. For a comparison of studies that employ administrative data and those that rely on surveys to estimate participation, see Carol Trippe, Pat Doyle, and Andrew Asher, *Trends in Food Stamp Program Participation Rates: 1976 to 1990* (Food and Nutrition Service, USDA, 1992), p. 6.

60. Carole Trippe and Julie Sykes, *Food Stamp Program Participation Rates, January 1992* (Food and Nutrition Service, USDA, 1994), p. 36.

61. Ibid., p. xiii.

62. Ibid. Among households entitled to $150 in stamps or more per month, participation is at 89 percent; when the expectation is less than $150, the rate falls to 55 percent. The average per capita monthly benefit in 1993 was $68, with a maximum allotment for a family of four of $375.

63. Ibid., pp. xi–xii, 7. These are all 1992 figures.

64. Alberto Martini, *Participation in the Food Stamp Program: A Multivariate Analysis* (Food and Nutrition Service, USDA, 1992), pp. xi–xii.

65. Ibid.

66. Nancy Burstein, *Dynamics of the Food Stamp Program as Reported in the Survey of Income and Program Participation* (Food and Nutrition Service, USDA, 1993), p. x.

67. Barbara Fay Murphy and Marielouise Harrell, *Characteristics of Long-Term Participants in the Food Stamp Program* (Food and Nutrition Service, USDA, 1992), p. 10.

68. Richard Coe, "A Longitudinal Analysis of Nonparticipation in the Food Stamp Program by Eligible Households," Discussion Paper 773-85 (Institute for Research on Poverty, University of Wisconsin–Madison, March 1985). See also Richard Coe, "Nonparticipation in Welfare Programs by Eligible Households: The Case of the Food Stamp Program," *Journal of Economic Issues*, vol. 17 (December 1983). See in addition studies summarized in Physician Task Force on Hunger in America, "Increasing Hunger and Declining Help: Barriers to Participation in the Food Stamp Program," Harvard School of Public Health, May 1986, pp. 62–64.

69. Coe, "A Longitudinal Analysis," p. 64.

70. Physician Task Force on Hunger in America, "Increasing Hunger and Declining Help," p. 59.

71. GAO, *Food Stamps: Reasons for Nonparticipation*, Report to the Ranking Minority Member, Subcommittee on Domestic Marketing, Consumer Relations, and Nutrition of the House Committee on Agriculture (GPO, 1988)

72. Ibid.

73. Darrell Hollonbeck and James Ohls, "Participation among the Elderly in the Food Stamp Program," *Gerontologist*, vol. 24 (December 1984), p. 618.

74. Although two-thirds of a public sample said they believed government should take care of people who can't take care of themselves (*New York Times*/CBS poll, February 1995), a majority of the public also believes that welfare encourages women to have children, fosters family breakup, and discourages the work ethic (*Los Angeles Times*, April 1994; and *Times Mirror* Poll, April 1995).

75. Congress amended the 1964 act in 1970 to require state outreach efforts. A summary of developments in food stamp outreach may be found in USDA, Food and Consumer Service, "A History of Outreach in the Food Stamp Program," n.d. See also MacDonald, *Food, Stamps, and Income Maintenance*, p. 91.

76. *Congressional Record*, June 8, 1973, p. 18840.

77. 386 F. Supp. 10–59 (C.D. Minn. 1974).

78. Confirmation that lack of information remains a major factor in limiting food stamp participation is contained in unpublished reports to USDA by small grant recipients. See, for example, Douglas Cherokee Economic Authority, "Food Stamp Outreach and Client Assistance in Rural Counties of Southeastern Appalachia," Morristown, Tennessee, October 1993–June 1995; Southern California Interfaith Hunger Coalition, "Reaccessing Los Angeles: Community Partners to Access Food," Los Angeles, September 1993–February 1995; and Project Bread, "USDA Food Stamp Client Enrollment Assistance Demonstration Project: Final Report," Boston, 1995. Gary Bickel of the Food and Consumer Service reports that "most states don't do outreach any more." Interview with the author, June 20, 1996.

79. Berry, *Feeding Hungry People*, pp. 27, 36.

80. *A Review of the Thrifty Food Plan and Its Use in the Food Stamp Program*, Report prepared by the Subcommittee on Domestic Marketing, Consumer Relations, and Nutrition of the House Committee on Agriculture (GPO, 1985), p. 1.

81. *Congressional Quarterly Weekly Report*, vol. 34 (February 21, 1976), p. 446.

82. John T. Cook, Laura Sherman, and J. Larry Brown, "Impact of Food Stamps on the Dietary Adequacy of Poor Children" (Center on Hunger, Poverty and Nutrition Policy, Tufts University, June 1995).

83. Barbara Devaney and Robert Moffitt, "Dietary Effects of the Food Stamp Program," *American Journal of Agricultural Economics*, vol. 73 (February 1991), pp. 202–11.

84. Ohls and Beebout, *The Food Stamp Program*, p. 170.

85. *Food Assistance in Rural Communities: Problems, Prospects, and Ideas from Urban Programs*, Hearing before the House Select Committee on Hunger, 102 Cong. 1 sess. (GPO, April 5, 1991), p. 70.

86. "Food Stamps Not Enough to Provide Adequate Diet," *Jet*, vol. 69 (November 1985), p. 28. See also *A Review of the Thrifty Food Plan and Its Use in the Food Stamp Program*, pp.13–14.

87. Ibid., p. 17.

88. The amount of the food stamp allotment is the difference between 30 percent of the household's cash income, after allowable deductions, and 100 percent of the cost of the Thrifty Food Plan. The 1996 law freezes the standard deduction at $134. If indexed, as it was before the 1996 reforms, it would have risen to $168 by 2002.

Chapter 5

1. See, for example, the congressional testimony of Arlene Zilke, a lobbyist for the National Parent Teacher Association. "When school lets out for the sum-

mer," she notes, "many children lose access to the one meal [school lunch] they had each day." Later she points out that "many school children depend on their day care providers for 75 to 80 percent of the nutrients they take in each day." *Hunger in America, Its Effects on Children and Families and Implications for the Future*, Hearing before the Subcommittee on Domestic Marketing, Consumer Relations, and Nutrition of the House Committee on Agriculture, 102 Cong. 1 sess. (GPO, May 8, 1991), pp. 231, 232.

2. In addition to the ongoing domestic programs listed in table 5-1, USDA's Food and Consumer Service administers a cash and coupon assistance program for Puerto Rico and the Northern Marianas, a pilot program that provides WIC participants with access to farmers markets (only eleven states took part in 1994) and disaster feeding, a commodity distribution program.

3. David Rush and others, "The National WIC Evaluation," *American Journal of Clinical Nutrition*, vol. 48 (August 1988), p. 389.

4. *To Save the Children*, Committee Print, Senate Select Committee on Nutrition and Human Needs (GPO, January 1974), p. 18. The staff authors claim that Freeman acted under pressure from the Poor People's Campaign, then demonstrating in Washington. See also National Advisory Council on Maternal, Infant, and Fetal Nutrition, *1980 Biennial Report* (GPO, 1980), p. 1. The Commodity Supplemental Food Program (CSFP) still operates, though only in eighteen states and the District of Columbia. It served nearly 400,000 people in 1996, compared with WIC's 7.4 million. CSFP provides USDA-purchased commodities, not always surplus, to low-income pregnant and lactating women, children up to six years of age, and elderly people. Concerns about overlap with the WIC program led the Reagan administration to propose wrapping both WIC and CSFP into a maternal and child health block grant in 1982, but Congress rejected the idea. CSFP offers a more varied package of supplemental foods than WIC, and because of USDA's bulk purchasing power, it costs less than WIC, whose recipients must use their coupons in retail outlets. See *Review of Commodity Supplemental Food Program*, Hearing before the Subcommittee on Domestic Marketing, Consumer Relations, and Nutrition of the House Committee on Agriculture, 97 Cong. 2 sess. (GPO, April 28, 1982).

5. Nutritional risk is defined as exhibiting abnormal nutritional conditions, documented nutritionally related medical conditions, health-impairing dietary deficiencies, or conditions that predispose people to inadequate nutrition. See *1996 Green Book*, Committee Print, House Committee on Ways and Means, 104 Cong. 2 sess. (GPO, 1996), p. 925.

6. This participation rate was fairly consistent over the life of the program prior to the 1990s. See *Role of Federal Food Assistance Programs in Strategies to Reduce Infant Mortality*, Hearing before the House Select Committee on Hunger, 100 Cong. 1 sess. (GPO, April 29, 1987), p. 35. A report by the Food Research and Action Center calculates that 62 percent of those between one and five years old who are poor and

nutritionally at risk, or about 3 million children, were not receiving WIC assistance in the 1980s. "WIC Misses Half of Eligible Population," *Social Policy*, vol. 21 (Winter 1990), p. 55.

7. *1996 Green Book*, Committee Print, pp. 927–28. The administration's estimate of the number of eligible applicants was 7.5 million. The slightly higher estimate of 8 million was made by the Congressional Budget Office.

8. Average monthly benefits in 1994 were $29.77. J. William Levedahl, "Annual Review of Domestic Food-Assistance Programs," *Food Review*, vol. 18 (May–August 1995), p. 33. Administrative costs amount to an additional $11 per participant.

9. *Maternal, Fetal, and Infant Nutrition–1973*, Hearing before the Senate Select Committee on Nutrition and Human Needs, 93 Cong. 1 sess. (GPO, December 6, 1973), p, 214.

10. Ibid., pp. 148–49.

11. *Maternal, Fetal, and Infant Nutrition–1973*, Hearing before the Senate Select Committee on Nutrition and Human Needs, 93 Cong. 1 sess. (GPO, June 7, 1973), p. 157.

12. Ibid., p. 158.

13. *Maternal, Fetal, and Infant Nutrition–1974*, Hearing before the Senate Select Committee on Nutrition and Human Needs, 93 Cong. 2 sess. (GPO, April 5, 1974), p. 311.

14. *To Save the Children*, Committee Print, p. 41.

15. *WIC and Commodity Supplemental Food Programs*, Hearing before the Senate Select Committee on Nutrition and Human Needs, 94 Cong. 2 sess. (GPO, March 30, 1976), p. 1.

16. Food and Nutrition Service, *Efficiency and Effectiveness in the WIC Program* (USDA, 1976). More recent data indicate that only 37 percent of WIC participants receive food stamps as well. USDA, "WIC Program and Participants Characteristics," April 1994.

17. *National WIC Evaluation: Reporting and Followup Issues*, Joint Hearing before the House Select Committee on Hunger and the Senate Committee on Agriculture, Nutrition, and Forestry, 101 Cong. 2 sess. (GPO, January 24, 1990), pp. 5, 9.

18. Ibid., p. 2.

19. Rush and others, "The National WIC Evaluation," p. 392.

20. *National WIC Evaluation*, Joint Hearing, p. 9.

21. Ibid. USDA officials referred to included a new management team in the Food and Consumer Service. Birge Watkins, a deputy assistant secretary, was the team's spokesperson in hearings before Congress.

22. *American Journal of Clinical Nutrition*, vol. 48, no. 2, supplement (August 1988).

23. At least one study, however, found no increase in total food expenditures among WIC participants, but the investigators did find that WIC influences food composition, reaffirming the early WIC evaluation conducted by the Urban Institute (Rush and others, "The National WIC Evaluation"). Gustavo Arcia, Luis Crouch, and Richard Kulka, "Impact of the WIC Program on Food Expenditures," *American Journal of Agricultural Economics*, vol. 72 (February 1990), p. 224.

24. Sheila Avruch and Alicia Puente Cackley, "Savings Achieved by Giving WIC Benefits to Women Prenatally," *Public Health Reports*, vol. 110 (January–February 1995), p. 29. Those studies that did not show significant differences tended to have very small sample sizes, one as low as seventy-nine.

25. GAO, *Early Intervention: Federal Investments Like WIC Can Produce Savings*, GAO/HRD-92-18 (April 1992), p. 5.

26. George Graham, "WIC: A Food Program That Fails," *Public Interest*, vol. 102 (Spring 1991), p. 76. The burden of Graham's attack is that the program was designed to combat a nonexistent problem—namely, malnutrition. It has instead contributed greatly to obesity among the poor by feeding them high fat, high cholesterol foods. In addition, although the rates of low birth weight and infant mortality have declined, they remain "scandalously" high, suggesting that WIC is ineffective.

27. *Role of Federal Food Assistance Programs in Strategies to Reduce Infant Mortality*, Hearing before the House Select Committee on Hunger, 100 Cong. 1 sess. (GPO, April 29, 1987), p. 4.

28. *Congressional Quarterly*, April 18, 1981, p. 666; and July 25, 1981, p. 1331.

29. Ibid., February 13, 1982, p. 242; September 18, 1982, p. 2343.

30. Gordon Gunderson, *The National School Lunch Program* (Food and Nutrition Service, USDA, 1971), pp. 5–7.

31. *Child Nutrition Programs: Issues for the 103rd Congress*, Committee Print, Subcommittee on Elementary, Secondary, and Vocational Education of the House Committee on Education and Labor, 103 Cong. 2 sess. (GPO, January, 1994), p. 40.

32. Current food assistance program data are on the USDA Web site at www.usda.gov.

33. Ardith Maney, *Still Hungry after All These Years: Food Assistance Policy from Kennedy to Reagan* (Greenwood, 1989), pp. 60–64; and GAO, *The Summer Feeding Program for Children: Reforms Begun—Many More Urgently Needed*, Report by the Comptroller General (GPO, 1978), p. 7.

34. *Oversight on the School Lunch Program*, Hearing before the Senate Committee on Agriculture, Nutrition, and Forestry, 102 Cong. 2 sess. (GPO, March 3, 1992), p. 24. Data for 1996 are on the USDA Web site at www.usda.gov.

35. *Congressional Quarterly*, July 25, 1981, p. 1331; and U.S. Congress, *Child Nutrition Programs: Issues for the 103rd Congress*, Committee Print, pp. 4–5.

36. GAO, *Participation in the National School Lunch Program*, Report to the Chairman, Senate Committee on Agriculture, Nutrition, and Forestry (GPO, March 20, 1984), p. 21.

37. *Child Nutrition Programs: Issues for the 103rd Congress*, Committee Print, pp. 4–5.

38. GAO, *Participation in the National School Lunch Program*, p. 23.

39. *Congressional Quarterly*, September 26, 1981, p. 1840.

40. The studies are described and the findings summarized in *Child Nutrition Programs: Issues for the 103rd Congress*, Committee Print, pp. 75–82.

41. Ibid., p. 75.

42. J. William Levedahl, Masao Matsumoto, and Mark Smith, "Food Assistance," *National Food Review*, vol. 13 (July–September 1990), p. 27.

43. About 2 percent of program funds are allocated for meals for disabled and elderly adults who live in adult day care settings.

44. *Child Nutrition Programs: Issues for the 103rd Congress*, Committee Print, p. 112.

45. Costs are given in 1995 dollars.

46. GAO, *The Summer Feeding Program—How to Feed the Children and Stop Program Abuses*, Report to the House Committee on Education and Labor (GPO, 1977), pp. 1–2.

47. GAO, *The Summer Feeding Program for Children*, p. 7.

48. *Child Nutrition Programs: Issues for the 103rd Congress*, Committee Print, p. 112.

49. GAO, *Food Assistance: Readmitting Private Nonprofit Sponsors into the Summer Food Service Program*, Report to Congressional Requesters (GPO, May 1991), pp. 2–3.

50. Michael Lipsky and Marc Thibodeau, "Feeding the Hungry with Surplus Commodities," *Political Science Quarterly*, vol. 103 (1988), p. 225.

51. In the late 1980s USDA estimated that 30 percent of all TEFAP commodities were distributed through nonprofit private food banks, a figure that suggests some important degree of interdependence between USDA and this sector of the social service infrastructure. *Food Bank Participation in the Temporary Emergency Food Assistance Program*, Hearing before the Subcommittee on Domestic Marketing, Consumer Relations, and Nutrition of the House Committee on Agriculture, 100 Cong. 1 sess. (GPO, May 29, 1987), p. 13. Second Harvest estimated that of the 700 million pounds of food it distributed to food banks in 1991, 124 million pounds, or about 18 percent, were federal commodities from TEFAP and what was then the separate soup kitchen/food bank commodities program. *USDA's Status of Commodity Supplies in the Emergency Food Assistance Program*

[TEFAP], Hearing before the Government Information, Justice, and Agriculture Subcommittee of the House Committee on Government Operations, 102 Cong. 2 sess. (GPO, June 17, 1992), p. 80.

52. Testimony of Chris Rebstock, Second Harvest, in U.S. Congress, *USDA's Status of Commodity Supplies in the Emergency Food Assistance Program [TEFAP]*, Hearing, pp. 80, 83.

53. Ibid., p. 85; and William Levedahl, Nicole Ballenger, and Courtney Harold, *Comparing the Emergency Food Assistance Program and the Food Stamp Program: Recipient Characteristics, Market Effects, and Benefit/Cost Ratios* (Economic Research Service, USDA, 1994), p. 1.

54. Ibid., p. 3.

55. *Food Bank Participation in the Temporary Emergency Food Assistance Program*, Hearing, p. 48.

56. See "Should Federal Food Assistance Programs Be Converted to Block Grants?" (Washington, D.C.: Center on Budget and Policy Priorities, January 27, 1995); "The Child Nutrition Block Grants" (Washington, D.C.: Center on Budget and Policy Priorities, April 10, 1995); and Consumers Union, *Hunger, the Food Stamp Program, and State Discretion* (Washington, D.C.: Consumers Union, July 1995).

Chapter 6

1. See, for example, Elizabeth Drew's analysis in "Going Hungry in America," *Atlantic*, vol. 222 (December 1968), p. 54. For a more detailed account, see Ardith Maney, *Still Hungry after All These Years: Food Assistance Policy from Kennedy to Reagan* (Greenwood, 1989), pp. 19–22.

2. *Congressional Record*, April 7, 1964, p. 7131.

3. Ibid., p. 187. See also John Kingdon, *Agendas, Alternatives, and Public Policies* (Scott, Foresman, 1984), p. 103.

4. Jeffrey Berry, *Feeding Hungry People* (Rutgers University Press, 1984), chapter 2.

5. Ardith Maney argues that after 1964 civil rights groups in the South had begun to pressure USDA to extend the food stamp program to sharecroppers operating in a cashless economy. But food assistance and hunger issues did not figure prominently in the federal War on Poverty programs associated with the Economic Opportunity Act of 1964. See Maney's account of the civil rights groups' contributions to the food assistance debate in *Still Hungry after All These Years*, chapter 5.

6. Congressional accounts of this Mississippi trip are contained, among other places, in *Hunger and Malnutrition in the United States*, Hearings before the Subcommittee on Employment, Manpower, and Poverty of the Senate Committee

on Labor and Public Welfare, 90 Cong. 2 sess. (GPO, May 23, 29; June 12, 14, 1968); and *Studies of Human Need*, Committee Print, Senate Select Committee on Nutrition and Human Needs (GPO, June 1972).

7. *Hunger and Malnutrition in America*, Hearings before the Subcommittee on Employment, Manpower, and Poverty of the Senate Committee on Labor and Public Welfare, 90 Cong. 1 sess. (GPO, 1967).

8. Maney, *Still Hungry after All These Years*, pp. 111–12.

9. Roger Cobb and Charles Elder, *Participation in American Politics: The Dynamics of Agenda-Building*, 2d ed. (Johns Hopkins University Press, 1983), p. 187.

10. Kingdon, *Agendas, Alternatives, and Public Policies*, pp. 129, 188–92.

11. Berry, *Feeding Hungry People*, p. 43.

12. This account comes from Arthur Schlesinger, *Robert Kennedy and His Times* (Houghton Mifflin, 1978), pp. 794–95 (emphasis added).

13. The text of the April 27, 1967, letter from the Subcommittee to President Johnson is contained in *Legislative History of the Select Committee on Nutrition and Human Needs*, Committee Print, Senate Select Committee on Nutrition and Human Needs (GPO, October 1976), p. 5.

14. The term is Schlesinger's. See *Robert Kennedy and His Times*.

15. Some well-known and influential select committees of the recent past include the Senate Select Committee on Presidential Campaign Activities (a Watergate committee), the House and Senate Select Committees on Secret Military Assistance to Iran and the Nicaraguan Opposition, and the Senate Select Ethics Committee, which dealt with the sexual harassment accusations against Senator Robert Packwood (R-Ore.). See also William Morrow, *Congressional Committees* (Scribner's, 1969), p. 36.

16. The point is made in *Legislative History of the Select Committee on Nutrition and Human Needs*, Committee Print, p. 56.

17. Ibid. p. 60.

18. Ibid., p. 50.

19. Ibid., pp. 135–36.

20. Kingdon, *Agendas Alternatives, and Public Policies*, p. 98.

21. *Legislative History of the Select Committee on Nutrition and Human Needs*, Committee Print, p. 114.

22. Ibid., p. 242. Senator McGovern admitted to "overoptimism" in thinking that the committee could accomplish its task in a year.

23. Ibid., p. 198.

24. Ibid., p. 238.

25. Ibid., p. 199.

26. Ibid., pp. 353–54. McGovern was concerned about rising food prices and possible shortages in some parts of the country, both brought about by fuel shortages resulting from the Arab oil embargo. Food prices had risen more than 20 percent in the course of a year, and McGovern worried about even higher rates of

increase in urban areas. *Legislative History of the Select Committee on Nutrition and Human Needs*, Committee Print, pp. 353–54.

27. Ibid., p. 393.

28. The reform plan was the product of hearings held by the Temporary Select Committee to Study the Senate Committee System, created in 1976 (S. Res. 109, March 30, 1976). The plan, which pointed out that the number of committee assignments for the average senator had grown from five in 1947 to twenty by 1976, was brought to the floor of the Senate nine months later (S. Res. 4, January 25, 1977). *Congressional Record*, February 2, 1977, p. 3264.

29. *New York Times*, editorial, February 2, 1977.

30. *Congressional Record*, February 2, 1977, p. 3256.

31. See *Legislative History of the Select Committee on Nutrition and Human Needs*, Committee Print, pp. 113–14, 238.

32. *Congressional Record*, February 2, 1977, p. 3260.

33. Ibid., p. 3257. For similar remarks by Senators McGovern and Don Reigle (D-Mich.), see ibid., February 3, 1977, pp. 3613, 3618.

34. Berry, *Feeding Hungry People*, p. 149.

35. *Hunger in America: Ten Years Later*, Hearing before the Subcommittee on Nutrition of the Senate Committee on Agriculture, 96 Cong. 1 sess. (GPO, April 30, 1979), pp. 1–2.

36. H. Res. 784, 95 Cong. 1 sess.; and S. Res. 271, 95 Cong. 1 sess.

37. International hunger issues dominated the testimony, for example, in hearings held before the House Committee on Agriculture. See *To Establish a Commission on Domestic and International Hunger and Malnutrition*, Hearing before the House Committee on Agriculture, 95 Cong. 1 sess. (GPO, October 20, 1977).

38. Executive Order 12078, September 5, 1978.

39. Presidential Commission on World Hunger, *Overcoming World Hunger: The Challenge Ahead* (GPO, March 1980).

40. Data on average monthly food stamp participation come from USDA, *Agricultural Statistics* (GPO, 1992), p. 478. Poverty statistics are from Bureau of the Census, *Statistical Abstract of the United States, 1994*, p. 475.

41. Physician Task Force on Hunger in America, *Hunger in America* (Wesleyan University Press, 1985), pp. 12–13.

42. Interviews with Max Finberg, October 28, 1993, and Marty Rendon, October 29, 1993.

43. *Congressional Record*, February 22, 1984, p. 2970.

44. Interview with Max Finberg, October 28, 1993.

45. Interview with Jennifer Coken, October 28, 1993.

46. *Congressional Record*, February 22, 1984, p. 2966.

47. Two of its major provisions were to increase the amount of shelter costs that poor families might deduct from their income, the effect of which would be to lower the amount of disposable income remaining and thereby increase food

stamps, and to increase the value of an automobile that food stamp recipients may own. The quotation comes from a fact sheet (undated) distributed by the Center on Hunger, Poverty and Nutrition Policy, Tufts University.

48. *Congressional Quarterly*, January 30, p. 207; February 20, p. 388; and March 20, 1993, p. 647.

49. *Washington Post*, April 29, 1993, p. 13A.

50. News release from Office of Rep. Tony Hall, "Congressional Hunger Center and Caucus," October 14, 1993.

51. Extended remarks of Rep. Gary Ackerman (D-N.Y.), *Congressional Record*, April 1, 1993, p. E877.

52. Rendon interview, October 29, 1993.

53. *Progress Report of the [House] Select Committee on Hunger*, 100 Cong. 2 sess. (GPO, 1988), p. 56.

54. *Progress Report of the [House] Select Committee on Hunger*, 102 Cong. 2 sess. (GPO, 1993), p. 51.

55. Finberg interview and Coken interview, October 28, 1993.

56. See discussion in chapter 7.

57. *Progress Report of the [House] Select Committee on Hunger*, 1993, p. 52.

58. The characterization is that of J. Larry Brown, director of the Tufts Center on Hunger, Poverty, and Nutrition Policy and one of the original conveners of the Medford group. *Hunger in America: Who Cares?* Hearing before the House Select Committee on Hunger, 102 Cong. 2 sess. (GPO, April 30, 1992), p. 9.

59. Ibid., p. 1.

60. President Nixon's White House Conference on Food, Nutrition, and Health, President Carter's Commission on World Hunger, and President Reagan's Task Force on Food Assistance are the relevant examples.

61. *Congressional Quarterly*, January 30, 1993, p. 207.

Chapter 7

1. Food groups also lobbied officials in the executive branch, particularly USDA, as Ardith Maney makes clear in *Still Hungry after All These Years: Food Assistance Policy from Kennedy to Reagan* (Greenwood, 1989). But the select committees not only offered an entrée to the policymaking process but a public forum as well.

2. Patricia Kutzner, "Thirty Years of Hunger Advocacy," in Bread for the World, *Hunger 1994: Transforming the Politics of Hunger* (Silver Spring, Md.: Bread for the World Institute, 1993), p. 85.

3. Their number is not great, and people active in the anti-hunger effort agree on which groups ought to be included. See David Beckmann's comments on

the small number of important advocacy groups in his "Introduction" to *Hunger 1994: Transforming the Politics of Hunger*, p. 6.

4. RESULTS is an acronym for Responsibility Ending Starvation Using Legislation, Trimtabbing, and Support. A trimtab is a small rudder found on the back of a larger rudder that makes turning a boat (or ship of state) easier. Presumably, the analogy is to small grassroots organizations, the focus of RESULTS' mobilization efforts. See Sam Harris, *Reclaiming Democracy* (Philadelphia: Camino Books, 1994).

5. "Prophetic justice" is a doctrine espoused by some Protestant, Catholic, and Jewish groups that holds that people serve God, as did the ancient prophets, by denouncing and then working against injustice, inequality, and oppression.

6. Interview with Patricia Bengston, March 23, 1995. Similar sentiments were expressed in interviews with leaders from FRAC, RESULTS, and Tufts. Interviews with Robert Fersh, October 29, 1993; Ed Cooney, October 29, 1993; Sam Harris, March 24, 1995; and J. Larry Brown, June 30, 1995.

7. With respect to food and hunger in the United States the relevant Catholic documents are the U.S. Bishops' pastoral letter, *Economic Justice for All: Pastoral Letter on Catholic Social Teaching and the U.S. Economy* (1986); and National Conference of Catholic Bishops, *Report of the Ad Hoc Task Force on Food, Agriculture, and Rural Concerns* (November 15, 1988).

8. Interview with Nancy Wisdo, March 24, 1995.

9. Share Our Strength provides grants to political action organizations in the anti-hunger movement, but it avoids direct political involvement. As one official in the organization explained, "Some of our reluctance to do direct advocacy has to do with our corporate sponsorship, mainly American Express. They don't want to support criticism of what the government has done or hasn't done. . . . We work hard to get money to people in need and to groups working for social justice." Interview with Phyllis Jones, March 24, 1995.

10. Interview with David Beckmann, March 23, 1995.

11. Interview with J. Larry Brown, June 30, 1995.

12. Interview with Richard Hoehn, March 23, 1995.

13. The Tufts Center's formal name is the Center on Hunger, Poverty and Nutrition Policy at Tufts University. FRAC's Director of Child Nutrition Programs comments that "low-income people have a right to food. It's the federal government's responsibility to make sure low-income people have access to food programs. . . . Private charity is inconsistent. There's not enough, and they don't always provide a balanced diet." Interview with Lynn Parker, October 29, 1993.

14. Fersh interview, October 29, 1993.

15. RESULTS founder Sam Harris took inspiration from the Bangladeshi Grameen Bank, which provides small loans to peasant entrepreneurs. Harris interview, March 25, 1995. Representative Tony Hall also pushed microenterprise legislation in his Freedom from Hunger omnibus bill.

16. Interview with Joe Wilson, March 24, 1995. Share Our Strength founder Billy Shore is quoted in the *Washington Post*: "I would hate to think that the goal of this [Share Our Strength] effort is a country of fully funded food banks" (November 2, 1993).

17. Cooney interview, October 29, 1993.

18. William P. Browne, "Organized Interests and Their Issue Niches: A Search for Pluralism in a Policy Domain," *Journal of Politics*, vol. 52 (May 1990), p. 477.

19. Second Harvest's strategic plan reflects this concern. "Competition with other nonprofits for funds will accelerate," the plan asserts. It thus becomes important to promote the Second Harvest name, for "brand integrity . . . will continue as a key reason for the food industry donating through Second Harvest." *Second Harvest Strategic Plan,* 1993. Monetary donations to human service organizations represent about 10 percent of all charitable giving by households in the United States. "Human services" include food pantries and other food assistance programs, but they also include United Way, Red Cross, YMCA, United Jewish Appeal, and other multiservice agencies. Human service recipients are a distant second to religious organizations in the competition for charity dollars. See Independent Sector, *Giving and Volunteering in the United States* (Washington, D.C.: Independent Sector, 1992), p. 36.

20. Most corporate giving comes not in the form of cash but in food donations to pantries and feeding centers. Interview with John Riggan, January 13, 1995.

21. Harris interview, March 24, 1995.

22. Brown interview, June 30, 1995.

23. The phrase is contained in a World Hunger Year brochure, "Why World Hunger Year?" (New York: World Hunger Year, n.d.)

24. The Center on Budget and Policy Priorities is a nonprofit, tax-exempt organization, but it is permitted to provide analyses and testimony at Congress's request. Its activities in assisting the executive branch in policy development are not considered lobbying by the Internal Revenue Service.

25. Center on Budget and Policy Priorities, *A Report on the 1993 Activities of the Center on Budget and Policy Priorities* (Washington, D.C.: May 1994), p. 6.

26. "Products and Distribution List" (Medford, Mass.: Tufts Center on Hunger, Poverty and Nutrition Policy, January 1 to June 15, 1995).

27. Center on Hunger, Poverty and Nutrition Policy, "The Link Between Nutrition and Cognitive Development in Children," (Medford, Mass.: Tufts University School of Nutrition, 1995); and John T. Cook and Katie Martin, "Differences in Nutrient Adequacy among Poor and Non-Poor Children" (Medford, Mass: Tufts Center on Hunger, Poverty and Nutrition Policy, March 1995).

28. Fersh interview, October 29, 1993.

29. Ibid.

30. J. Larry Brown gives credit for the idea of the Medford Declaration to the head of the Maine Hunger Coalition, Bill Whitaker. Brown interview, June 30, 1995.

31. The text of the Medford Declaration and an explanation of its origins and uses is published by the Tufts Center in a glossy brochure dated December 1991.

32. Jean Dimeo, "Mayors Push Hunger Declaration," *American City & County*, vol. 107 (June 1992), p. 12.

33. Brown interview, June 30, 1995.

34. Beckmann interview, March 23, 1995.

35. Medford Group Conference Call Agenda, November 30, 1994, Tufts Center archives. Participants are listed on the agenda and include leaders from Share Our Strength, Second Harvest, World Hunger Year, Children's Defense Fund, Tony Hall's Congressional Hunger Center, Catholic Charities USA, RESULTS, and the U.S. Conference of Mayors.

36. Memo from J. Larry Brown to Medford Steering Committee on USDA Hunger Forum, May 28, 1993, Tufts Center archives.

37. Brown interview, June 30, 1995.

38. Memo from J. Larry Brown to State Hunger and Poverty Leaders, "Federal Nutrition Cuts and Welfare 'Reform'," November 30, 1994, Tufts Center archives.

39. Émile Durkheim, *The Division of Labor in Society* (Glencoe, Ill.: Free Press, 1960), p. 62. Durkheim also writes: "Society becomes more capable of collective movement at the same time that each of its elements has more freedom of movement" (p. 131).

Chapter 8

1. Second Harvest feeding programs collectively receive 55 percent of their income for operating expenses and food purchases from federal, state, and local governments. Voluntary contributions from individuals provide about 21 percent, while businesses donate no more than 5 percent. The balance is made up by United Way, churches, client fees, and foundations. *Second Harvest 1993 National Research Study* (Chicago: Second Harvest, 1993), p. 59.

2. Irene Glasser, *More Than Bread: Ethnography of a Soup Kitchen* (University of Alabama Press, 1988), p. 26; also, interview with Augusta Hamel, Second Harvest, July 9, 1997. The proportion of food distributed that comes from the federal government had dropped to 13.4 percent in 1995 from 22.2 percent in 1991.

3. Lester Salamon, James Musselwhite Jr., and Alan Abramson, "Voluntary Organizations and the Crisis of the Welfare State" (Urban Institute, October 1983), pp. 24, 28.

4. Richard Hoehn, "Religious Communities Respond to Hunger," *Hunger 1994: Transforming the Politics of Hunger* (Silver Spring, Md.: Bread for the World Institute, 1993), p. 40.

5. Aside from the major national anti-hunger organizations, most 501(C)(3) organizations are food banks and gleaning operations. Both these types of organizations play what is best described as a wholesaling role. Food banks collect donated bulk and raw food from public and private sources or purchase food outright from gift or grant funds and distribute it to street-level direct service agencies, such as pantries or soup kitchens. Gleaning operations, such as Foodchain or CityHarvest (New York City), collect prepared and perishable food, often left over from banquets or restaurants or supermarkets, which they distribute to soup kitchens or congregate feeding centers. Food pantries serve clients directly by distributing food that people take home to prepare. Soup kitchens prepare and serve meals that people eat on-site.

6. The most recent data on the finances of charitable organizations are, as Independent Sector says, "circa 1992." Information is based on reports to the Internal Revenue Service from 1,176 tax-exempt food distribution organizations. Independent Sector, *Nonprofit Almanac, 1996–1997* (Jossey-Bass, 1996). See also *Nonprofit Almanac, 1993–1994* for an earlier (1988) data set.

7. David Beckmann, "Introduction," *Hunger 1994*, p. 2.

8. Interview with Augusta Hamel, Second Harvest, July 9, 1997.

9. Richard Hoehn, "Feeding People—Half of Overcoming Hunger," *Hunger 1994*, p. 12.

10. *Second Harvest 1993 National Research Study*, p. 37.

11. The poll is cited in *Hunger in America: Who Cares?* Hearing before the House Select Committee on Hunger, 102 Cong. 2 sess. (GPO, April 30, 1992), p. 52. The poll was conducted by Vincent Breglio and funded by Kraft General Foods on behalf of the sponsors of the Medford Declaration.

12. Independent Sector, *Giving and Volunteering* (Washington, D.C.: Independent Sector, 1992). These data suggest that 94.2 million Americans volunteer in some capacity each year.

13. *Second Harvest 1993 National Research Study*, p. 72.

14. Michael Lipsky, "Federal Surplus Commodity Distribution to Households and Individuals: A Preliminary Assessment," Report prepared for the House Select Committee on Hunger, *Effective Uses of Agricultural Abundance for Hunger Relief*, 98 Cong. 2 sess. (GPO, September 20, 1984), pp. 206, 208.

15. Hoehn, "Feeding People—Half of Overcoming Hunger," p. 15; and *Child Nutrition Programs: Issues for the 103rd Congress*, Committee Print, Subcommittee on Elementary, Secondary, and Vocational Education of the House Committee on Education and Labor, 103 Cong. 2 sess. (GPO, January 1994), p. 113.

16. Salamon, Musselwhite, and Abramson, "Voluntary Organizations and the Crisis of the Welfare State," p. 28.

17. Burton Weisbrod, *The Nonprofit Economy* (Harvard University Press, 1988), p. 130.

18. *Second Harvest 1993 National Research Study*, p. 72.

19. See Benjamin Gidron, Ralph Kramer, and Lester Salamon, "Government and the Third Sector in Comparative Perspective: Allies or Adversaries?" in Gidron, Kramer, and Salamon, eds., *Government and the Third Sector* (Jossey-Bass, 1992), p. 19. The authors speak of two models of government and third-sector relations, both of which apply to the food assistance system. One is a collaborative model in which government provides the financing and the third sector delivers the services. The other is the so-called dual model in which the third sector fills needs not met by government programs.

20. Beth Osborne Daponte, "Private versus Public Relief: Utilization of Food Pantries versus Food Stamps among Poor Households in Allegheny County, Pennsylvania," Discussion Paper 1091-96 (Institute for Research on Poverty, University of Wisconsin–Madison, 1996).

21. Patricia K. Smith and Sharon L. Hoerr, "A Comparison of Current Food Bank Users, Non-Users and Past Users in a Population of Low Income Single Mothers," *Journal of Nutrition Education*, vol. 24 (January–February Supplement, 1992), p. 60S.

22. *Second Harvest 1993 National Research Study*, p. 156.

23. Ibid., pp. 153–58.

24. Glasser, *More Than Bread*, p. 22.

25. Gidron, Kramer, and Salamon, "Government and the Third Sector in Comparative Perspective," p. 6.

26. Interview with Gail Nix, Dane County (Wisconsin) Community Action Commission, April 29, 1997.

27. Raw data supplied to the author by Community Action Coalition of South Central Wisconsin.

28. Daponte, "Private versus Public Relief," p. 3.

29. Lipsky, "Federal Surplus Commodity Distribution to Households and Individuals," p. 210.

30. Cruz Torres, Mary Zey, and William Alex McIntosh, "Effectiveness in Voluntary Organizations: An Empirical Assessment," *Sociological Focus*, vol. 24 (August 1991), pp. 157–67; and Cruz Torres, William Alex McIntosh, and Mary Zey, "The Effects of Bureaucratization and Commitment on Resource Mobilization in Voluntary Organizations," *Sociological Spectrum*, vol. 11 (1991), pp. 19–44.

31. See, for example, the analysis of Bill Shore, founder of Share Our Strength, in his *Revolution of the Heart* (New York: Riverhead Books, 1995), p. 100.

32. The passage that follows is based on the report by John T. Cook and J. Larry Brown, "Analysis of the Capacity of the Second Harvest Network To Cover the Federal Food Stamp Shortfall from 1997 to 2002" (Center on Hunger, Poverty and Nutrition Policy, Tufts University, July 1997).

33. House Select Committee on Hunger, *Food Security in the United States*, Committee Report, October 1990, p. 19.

34. Jan Poppendieck, "Dilemmas of Emergency Food: A Guide for the Perplexed" (Hunter College Center for the Study of Family Policy, Summer 1992), p. 6.

35. *Congressional Record*, April 7, 1964, p. 7142.

36. GAO, *Surplus Commodities: Temporary Emergency Food Assistance Program's Operations and Continuance* (GPO, 1987).

37. Robert Wuthnow, *Acts of Compassion: Caring for Others and Helping Ourselves* (Princeton University Press, 1991).

38. *Second Harvest 1993 National Research Study*, p. 36.

39. Glasser, *More Than Bread*, pp. 21–22.

40. Ibid., pp. 29, 140.

41. Interview with Gail Nix, July 16, 1997.

42. Ibid.

43. Interview with Doug O'Brien, Second Harvest, July 16, 1997.

44. Hoehn, "Religious Communities Respond to Hunger," p. 35.

45. Glasser, *More Than Bread*, p. 148.

46. Ibid., pp. 28, 29, 143. Toward the end of Glasser's multiyear period of observation, the soup kitchen hired a professional nutritionist to plan menus.

47. Poppendieck, "Dilemmas of Emergency Food," p. 6.

48. Ibid., p. 7.

49. Cathy Campbell, "Private Food Assistance: The Emerging Third Tier of Our Food Distribution System," *New York's Food and Life Sciences Quarterly*, vol. 20 (1990), p. 41.

50. These states may, of course, have other food banks, but Second Harvest banks are typically the best connected and best supported of such institutions.

51. This is one way to explain Karen Curtis's finding that many volunteers in soup kitchens continue to provide service but actually doubt the claims of need by many clients. "Urban Poverty and the Social Consequences of Privatized Food Assistance," *Journal of Urban Affairs*, vol. 19 (1997), p. 217.

52. Mary Douglas, "Standard Social Uses of Food: Introduction," in Mary Douglas, ed., *Food in the Social Order* (Russell Sage, 1984), p. 10.

53. Shore, *Revolution of the Heart*, p. 114.

54. Independent Sector, *Giving and Volunteering*, p. 223.

Chapter 9

1. H.R. 1507 called for indexing the standard deduction for food stamp recipients to the Consumer Price Index, increasing the excess shelter deduction, increasing WIC funding to accommodate the entire eligible caseload, restoring

cuts in summer food service, providing outreach support to encourage schools to enroll in school breakfast, increasing funding for TEFAP and for an additional snack for children in day care, among other changes.

2. Food assistance policy changes effected by PRWORA are summarized in Joe Richardson, *Food Stamp Reform: The Continuing Debate*, CRS Report for Congress (Congressional Research Service, June 20, 1997). Able-bodied adults between the ages of 18 and 50 who have no dependents are ineligible if they received food stamps for three months within the previous thirty-six months while not working at least twenty hours a week or taking part in a certified work training program. Under certain circumstances, such people may come back on the food stamp rolls for another three months, for a total of six months in any thirty-six-month period. All legal immigrants were initially barred by PRWORA from participating unless they were political asylees or had a substantial history of work coverage under social security. Congress restored eligibility to about 250,000 children, elderly, and handicapped immigrants in the summer of 1998. The average monthly food stamp caseload was estimated to decline by 1 million persons because of the able-bodied rule and, after restoration to certain categories of legal immigrants, by another roughly 650,000.

3. Ibid., p. 3. The 1996 law cuts $54 billion over six years from various welfare programs. The reduction in the food stamp allotment will save $6 billion. The food stamp program targets the very poor: more than half of all participating households in 1992 had incomes below 50 percent of the poverty line.

4. Center on Budget and Policy Priorities, "Discussion of Selected Food Stamp Provisions in the Personal Responsibility Act" (Washington, D.C.: Center on Budget and Policy Priorities, April 7, 1995).

5. On state cashout and electronic card experiments, see USDA, Food and Nutrition Service, *New Directions in Food Stamp Policy Research*, Papers presented at the Food and Nutrition Service Research Conference, Washington, D.C., June 25, 1993. The inequities produced by decentralized control over the program in the early 1970s are documented in Consumers Union, *Hunger, the Food Stamp Program, and State Discretion* (Washington, D.C.: Consumers Union, July 1995).

6. On the debate over whether food stamps should function as an income transfer, which makes it difficult to justify stamps or vouchers, or a food program, for which stamps are appropriate, see R. Shep Melnick, *Between the Lines: Interpreting Welfare Rights* (Brookings, 1994), pp. 189ff.

7. Carol Olander, "Electronic Benefit Transfer in the Food Stamp Program: The First Decade," *New Directions in Food Stamp Policy Research*, pp. 101–16.

8. Burton Weisbrod, "The Future of the Nonprofit Sector: Its Entwining with Private Enterprise and Government," *Journal of Policy Analysis and Management*, vol. 16 (Fall 1997), pp. 541–55.

9. *Second Harvest 1993 National Research Study* (Chicago: Second Harvest, 1993), p. 156.

10. Food and Consumer Service, *Household Food Security in the United States in 1995: Summary Report of the Food Security Measurement Project* (USDA, September 1997), p. 55.

11. *Urban Grocery Gap*, Hearing before the House Select Committee on Hunger, 102 Cong. 2 sess. (GPO, September 30, 1992), p. 1.

12. James M. McDonald and Paul Nelson, "Do the Poor Still Pay More? Food Price Variations in Large Metropolitan Areas," *Journal of Urban Economics*, vol. 30 (1991), pp. 353, 357.

13. *Urban Grocery Gap*, Hearing, p. 17.

14. Michael Porter, "New Strategies for Inner-City Economic Development," *Economic Development Quarterly*, vol. 11 (February 1997), pp. 11–27.

15. McDonald and Nelson, "Do the Poor Still Pay More?" This study found that insurance costs were on average 64 percent higher for stores in inner cities.

16. The city of Hartford, Connecticut, has used Community Development Block Grant funds and vacant city-owned land to help private operators develop grocery stores. *Urban Grocery Gap*, Hearing, p. 22. See also Geoffrey Baker, *Food Marketing in the Inner City: Trends and Options*, CRS Report for Congress (Congressional Research Service, September 24, 1992).

17. McDonald and Nelson, "Do the Poor Still Pay More?" p. 349.

18. James Welsh, "Geosocial Thinking for the Food Stamp Program," *New Directions in Food Stamp Policy Research*, p. 135.

19. *Urban Grocery Gap*, Hearing, p. 1.

20. *Household Food Insecurity*, p. 45.

Index